DISORDERED WORLD

Setting a New Course
for the Twenty-first Century

AMIN MAALOUF

Translated from the French by George Miller

B L O O M S B U R Y
LONDON · BERLIN · NEW YORK · SYDNEY

First published in Great Britain 2011

Copyright © Editions Grasset & Fasquelle 2009
English translation copyright © George Miller 2011

'The Orchestra' by William Carlos Williams, from *The Collected Poems:
Volume II, 1939–1962*, copyright © 1948, 1962 by William Carlos Williams.
Reprinted by permission of New Directions Publishing Corp.

Bloomsbury Publishing Plc
50 Bedford Square
London
WC1B 3DP

www.bloomsbury.com

Bloomsbury Publishing, London, Berlin, New York and Sydney
A CIP catalogue record for this book is available from the British Library

ISBN 978 1 4088 1598 4

10 9 8 7 6 5 4 3 2 1

Typeset by Hewer Text UK Ltd, Edinburgh
Printed in Great Britain by Clays Ltd, St Ives plc

MIX
Paper from
responsible sources
FSC
www.fsc.org   FSC® C018072

For Marlène and Salim Nasr
And in memory of Paolo Vida (1948–2005)

Man has survived hitherto
because he was too ignorant to know
how to realize his wishes.
Now that he can realize them,
he must either change them
or perish.

from 'Orchestra',
William Carlos Williams,
Collected Poems (1954)

CONTENTS

Preface to the English Edition   xi

Preface to the Original Edition   xxi

   I   Misleading Victories   1

  II   Lost Legitimacy   69

III   Imaginary Certainties   153

      Afterword   231

      Bibliography   251

Preface to the English Edition

I thought it useful to write a preface to this edition, because the thesis at the heart of this book suddenly, and spectacularly, appeared at the very front of the world stage in the early months of 2011 – and seems likely to remain there for some time to come.

In examining what I have called a 'disordered world', I came to the conclusion that one of the roots of the problem was that leaders of the Arab world lacked legitimacy in the eyes of their people. Deprived of freedom, dignity, a future and the revenues their countries have earned from oil and other natural resources which have been misappropriated by ruling families, many Arabs had succumbed to despair, to the point of contemplating suicide. There is scarcely any need to mention that extremists have profited from this state of mind to recruit militants ready to become suicide bombers.

Paradoxically, the Arab spring also began with suicides. But in this case they had a very different political and ethical meaning: they were not acts of murder but self-sacrifice in the manner of the Buddhist monks who set fire to themselves in Vietnam in the 1960s. A man prepared to die for a cause becomes a powerful weapon, and the Arabs have

discovered that this weapon is infinitely more effective when
it ceases to be destructive, hate-filled and murderous, and is
instead put to the service of universally recognised values –
liberty, democracy, integrity, transparency and the right of
every human being to dignity and a decent life.

'Yes, we are desperate,' countless Arab protesters said
through their actions. 'Yes, we are ready to sacrifice ourselves,
but we will die like saints, like true martyrs, not like
murderers. We will not kill and we will not destroy.'
'Salmiyah!' ('We are peaceful!') the demonstrators chanted
every time anger levels rose, in order to calm their opponents and moderate their fellow protesters. 'No violence!
We want only to live, to be able to express ourselves freely,
to sing, and to connect with the rest of the world like young
Europeans and Americans and all other peoples. We are heirs
to a great civilisation and deserve the best.'

From the first uprisings, the crowd chanted famous lines
by the Tunisian poet Aboul-Qacem Echebbi:

> If the people one day desire life
> It is inevitable that destiny grants it
> It is inevitable that the darkness lifts . . .

The desire for life and preference for non-violent action
were to remain a deep inspiration to the movement. In this
sense, the Arab spring of 2011 represents the most eloquent
– and in the long run the most effective – riposte to the
attacks of 11 September 2001 and the jihadist ideology which
inspired them.

Long before Osama bin Laden collapsed in a hail of US

commando bullets in his compound in Abbottabad in May 2011, his strategy had already collapsed in the streets of Arab towns. He himself implicitly recognised this in his last statement, which was disseminated shortly after his death and differed in both tone and content from his previous pronouncements: making no mention of the armed struggle, he spoke bizarrely of representative assemblies and research institutes, and concluded with a saying of the Prophet which states that the most venerable of martyrs are those who stand up to authority to accuse them and those who are killed for their courage in speaking out.

Of course, terrorism such as we have seen since the start of this century will not disappear overnight; for some time to come it will retain its power to do harm. But for the people in whose name it claims to speak, it has now been consigned to the past. In overcoming their fear of dictators, the Arabs have overcome their indulgence towards terrorists.

Under autocratic rule, militant extremists were sometimes like fish in water. Their acts, however absurd, seemed a plausible response to the atmosphere of despair; and for lack of any alternative, many were willing to support them. Today, millions of men and women can hold their heads high and say that they themselves are heroes; they defied dictatorships, braved police repression, stood directly in the line of fire and helped liberate their people without soiling their hands or blackening their souls.

Up until recently, the Arab world had been caught in the crossfire of two groups of usurpers: those who seized power and wealth in the name of the nation or a dynasty, or in the name of stability and the fight against extremists; and those who invoked the name of Islam to advance their own intolerant, regressive political agenda.

What is more, these two types of usurpation reinforced each other. Under the pretext of fighting terrorism, autocrats won recognition, help and support; when the level of this support sometimes flagged, some regimes had no compunction about committing terrorist attacks themselves, which they attributed to the Islamists, so as to appear as a useful bulwark to the international community. The debate over whether it was religious fanatics or state agents who bombed such and such a church, carried out a particular massacre or assassinated a certain individual will last a long time.

The whole world seemed to believe that this perverse status quo would last for ever. How could it not, it was said, since the people themselves are resigned to it? But the people's patience was not infinite.

The signal for the great uprising was given by a young Tunisian street vendor, Mohammed Bouazizi, who set fire to himself after a municipal official slapped him in public and confiscated his vegetable cart. He died after eighteen days of agony on 4 January 2011. His act of despair was seen by his compatriots as a reflection of their own. 'But,' they reasoned, 'if we are prepared to die, what is the sense of each of us dying in our own little corner? Why not march against those who oppress and terrorise us? We may well be arrested and beaten, even gunned down in our tens or hundreds, but at least we will have the satisfaction of dying with our heads held high, trying to bring down tyrants.'

When, faced with this unexpected determination, the authorities seemed to hesitate, retreat or waver, it was initially a marvellous surprise and a terrific incentive for the protesters to go all the way – first in Tunisia, then in Egypt and then in other countries. More mass demonstrations sprang up, as did clashes with the security forces. And established regimes, which were hated by their people and had held on to their power for decades through intimidation and terror, began to crumble one after the other like rotting edifices: Zine-el-Abidine Ben Ali left Tunis on 14 January, twenty-three years after the coup d'etat that brought him to power; Hosni Mubarak left Cairo on 11 February, in the thirtieth year of his presidency. The movement soon sent shock waves of varying intensity through various Arab regimes.

After these first dazzling successes, there was a feeling that peaceful protest was going to have an almost miraculous domino effect throughout the entire region, linked in part to new means of communication – Facebook, Twitter, YouTube, smartphones, etc. – which would accelerate and amplify the movement, giving it a resonance among both local populations and international opinion. But subsequent events soon tempered that initial euphoria.

The turning point came first in Libya. Demonstrations began in Benghazi on 15 February and rapidly spread throughout the country. Up until then, Colonel Muammar Gaddafi, who had been in power for almost forty-two years, seemed immoveable. So it was astonishing to see a scenario similar to those in Tunisia and Egypt beginning to be played out there, too. Of course, from its earliest days it was violently repressed, creating hundreds of victims, but the protests kept on growing and by the end of that week speculation had begun as to the likely destination for the exile of the soon-to-be-ousted dictator. There were persistent rumours that he was already on his way to Venezuela.

This was premature. At the critical point at which Ben Ali and Mubarak judged it futile to hang on and thought it better to go, Gaddafi dug his heels in. Of course, he was different from his neighbours in many ways – his personality, the structure of his regime, the topography of his country – but the most significant distinguishing feature at that crucial moment was linked to the nature of Libya's armed forces. In both Tunisia and Egypt, the regular army had not wanted to fire on civilians, leaving that degrading task to the police and special forces; in Libya, the regular army carried little weight and the best-armed, most combat-hardened contingents reported directly to Gaddafi and his sons; he decided therefore to use them to the limit and turn all their fire power on the demonstrators. That allowed him to retake Tripoli and then launch a recovery operation throughout the country. Confronted with an organised military offensive, peaceful marching in the streets and public squares no longer made any sense. Protesters seized weapons they found in the barracks in their towns, thereby becoming insurgents. A civil war had begun that would soon lead to international intervention.

This escalation in the violence had repercussions elsewhere in the region, where several rulers felt that they could avoid being overthrown by clinging on to power, cracking down more severely, and ignoring the demands of their people and the condemnation of the international community. There were, of course, major differences between the Libyan situation and those of other countries such as Yemen,

Bahrain and Syria, but it became clear from the first weeks of the year that peaceful protests would not be enough to bring down Arab regimes, and that they would fight fiercely – even savagely – to ensure their survival.

As I write this preface, the initial revolutionary wave seems to have run out of steam, and the pace of dramatic change, which was gathering momentum from week to week, or to be exact from one Friday to the next, now seems to stretch over months and even years. Where the movement has already won victories, it has quickly reached the difficult and thankless phase of reconstruction. New democratic institutions need to be established, economies restarted, social tensions managed – and all this in countries where the people's expectations are huge and no leadership has emerged. This is because what constitutes the revolutionary movements' strength – their spontaneity, the key role played by idealistic, imaginative and generally non-partisan young people – also constitutes their weakness. Those who fought on the internet, making good use of social networks and skilfully circumventing official censorship to put up videos showing the security forces' brutality, succeeded as if by a miracle in sweeping away the regimes in power; but they were not able to transform themselves into governments or administrators. They had no option but to leave power in the hands of the military and experienced politicians who had distanced themselves – sometimes very late in the day – from the fallen despots, but who did not necessarily share the ideals of the rebellious young people. As a result, it is hardly surprising that the transition is turning out to be long, faltering, troubled and littered with pitfalls.

Will Egypt, the most populous Arab country and the one which in the past has often been their leader, especially at the time of Gamal Abdel Nasser, be able to assume political, economic and social leadership once more? Will it be able to construct a stable democracy, catch up in the field of education, define the place of religion in public life, manage relations between different communities, and give women full rights? And will Tunisia, which was the pioneer in the great uprising and which has always been at the vanguard of social modernity in the Arab world, be able to come up with an advanced model that will inspire other countries?

On this as on so many other scores, it would be presumptuous to make predictions. If there is a lesson to be drawn from the events of 2011, it is that the future does not allow itself to be contained within the limits of what is foreseeable, plausible or probable. And it is precisely for that reason that it contains hope.

While nations which have already freed themselves get down to the difficult task of transition, the struggle against dictatorial powers is proceeding at different speeds in the rest of the Middle East and North Africa. In some countries, leaders seem irredeemably weakened both domestically and internationally, and it is conceivable that when the protesters triumph, it will give the whole of the Arab uprising a new impetus. Because even if the resilience of regimes has been strengthened, the people's determination has not been broken, despite bloody repression.

All the ingredients of the initial revolt are still present, apart from the element of surprise. The causes of unhappiness have not, of course, disappeared – quite the reverse. Fearful despots behave with more ferocity than ever, thereby losing what little legitimacy they had retained in the eyes of their subjects, who now regard them more as foreign occupiers than as national leaders. And any moves towards reform on the part of most of these regimes remain timid, often no more than vague promises intended to calm the protesters' passion while waiting for the storm to pass so that business as usual can be resumed.

And yet, in people's minds, a great deal has changed, though those in power often fail to realise how profoundly. All Arab societies have shown a deep desire to live with dignity and a remarkable determination to fight to achieve it. It has often been said during this turbulent period that the Arabs have put an end to the myth which suggests they are less hungry for freedom than other peoples and less keen to live in representative democracies. This myth has effectively collapsed, but what has happened goes much further than that. The Arabs have not just caught up; they have not simply joined the group of democratic peoples: they have gone much further. 2011 will not just go down in history as the Arab equivalent of 1989 in Central and Eastern Europe. At no point in recent history – not even at the fall of the Berlin Wall – have we seen tens of millions of people brave death, baring their chests to bullets, and growing neither tired nor discouraged, as we have seen in Taez, Zawiya, Manama or Homs, day after day, week after week. Nowhere in the world have we seen such heroism. It is an exceptional, unprecedented phenomenon, and perhaps the harbinger of a democratic renewal worldwide.

The German poet Hölderlin said: 'Where there is danger, some salvation grows there too.' The great uprising of the Arab people bears out his words. For my part, I would add:

it is from those places where the world has been most disordered that in the next few decades the readjustment could
come. So that a planet which is more peaceful, harmonious
and human might be born, and therefore one which is more
capable of facing the common dangers that lie ahead.

Amin Maalouf
Paris, 31 May 2011

Postscript

Rereading the pages that follow, I realised there were many
things I would have written differently today, not so much at
the level of fact, but certainly of tone. For while my diagnosis remains roughly the same, my state of mind has
undoubtedly changed. That 'Arab despair' which I describe
at length, I was experiencing it myself; I certainly did not
relate to the suicidal and regressive reactions which that
despair had triggered; and although I hoped for some kind of
democratic uprising, I did not believe it would come so
quickly. After pondering at length whether I should alter the
text in the light of recent facts, I decided not to do so – or
only very little. It seemed to me that, in both its analysis and
its tone, this essay represents a faithful image of the state of
mind which led to the spectacular events we have witnessed,
and that it might provide a useful perspective for understanding what happened and what could still happen. I
therefore chose not to make too many changes and have
limited any substantial additions to the Preface to the English
Edition and the Afterword.

Preface to the Original Edition

We have embarked on this century without a compass.

From its very first months, disturbing events took place which created the impression that the world had gone seriously off course in several areas at once – it had gone off course intellectually, financially, environmentally, geopolitically and ethically.

It is true that from time to time upheavals occur which bring unexpected benefits. At such times we may begin to believe that when humanity gets itself into an impasse, it will inevitably find its way out by some miracle. But soon after, other kinds of turbulence come along which reveal quite different human impulses – darker, more familiar ones – prompting one to wonder if our species has reached its threshold of moral incompetence, and whether humanity is still advancing, or has in fact gone into reverse, threatening to undermine all that countless previous generations worked to build.

To avoid any misunderstanding, let me emphasise that I am not one of those people who want nothing to do with the modern world. I am fascinated by what our age has to offer. I eagerly await the latest inventions and am quick to adopt them. I am conscious of belonging to a generation that is highly privileged compared to every previous one, if only by dint of advances in medicine and information technology. But I cannot calmly enjoy the benefits of modernity if I am uncertain that generations to come will be able to enjoy them just as much.

Are these fears disproportionate? Sadly, I don't think so. In fact, they strike me as fully justified, as I will try to show in this book. I shall do so not in order to accumulate a mass of evidence, nor to defend my belief out of vanity but simply so that my cry of alarm is heard. My main aim is to find a way to persuade my contemporaries, my travelling companions, that the ship we find ourselves aboard has gone adrift. It is off course. It has no destination and no compass, and it is hard to see the way ahead on a stormy sea. Emergency action is required if we are to avoid shipwreck. It is no longer enough to stick to our current course, for better or worse, somehow navigating by sight, avoiding obstacles as they rear up and leaving it to time. Time is not on our side; it is our judge, and a suspended sentence has already been pronounced.

If maritime images come to mind spontaneously, perhaps I should first make my fears explicit with this simple, clear assessment: at the present point in our evolution, humanity faces new dangers never before encountered in our history. They call for unprecedented global solutions. If they are not found in the near future, it will not be possible to save any of the things which give our civilisation its greatness and beauty. Yet to date there are few indications that

provide reason to hope that humanity will be able to overcome its differences, devise imaginative solutions and put
them into effect. There are many signs that suggest that the
world is so severely out of joint that decline will be hard to
prevent.

In the pages that follow, I shall not treat each different form
of disorder systematically or as a separate case study. My
approach will rather be that of a nightwatchman in a garden
in the small hours after a storm when another more violent
storm looms on the horizon. With his lantern, this man carefully picks his way, shining its beam first on one flower bed,
then another, exploring one path, then retracing his steps
and bending over to inspect an old uprooted tree. Then he
makes for a promontory, puts out his light and tries to take
in the whole scene.

He is neither botanist, nor crop specialist, nor landscape
gardener, and nothing in the garden belongs to him personally. But this is where he lives with people he cares about,
and everything which might affect this land matters greatly
to him.

I

Misleading Victories

I

When the Berlin Wall fell, a hopeful breeze blew across the world. The end of the stand-off between the West and the Soviet Union removed the threat of a nuclear cataclysm which had hung over our heads for forty years. We believed that democracy would now gradually spread until it encompassed the whole planet; the barriers between countries would fall; the movement of people, goods, images and ideas would develop unimpeded, ushering in an era of progress and prosperity. On each of these fronts there were some remarkable advances to begin with. But the further we went, the more disorientated we became.

An example of this confusion is the European Union. For the EU, the disintegration of the Soviet bloc was a triumph. One of the two paths offered to the continent's peoples had turned out to be a dead end, while the other opened onto new horizons. All the former countries of the East came knocking at the EU's door, and those which were turned away still dream of being admitted. And yet, at the very moment of its triumph, when so many peoples were gravitating towards it in a kind of dazed fascination as though it were an earthly paradise, Europe lost its bearings. What was it supposed to be a union *of*? And what was its purpose? Who should it exclude and on what grounds? Now more than ever, the EU is questioning its identity, its borders, its future institutions, its place in the world. And it is not clear what the answers are.

If the EU understands perfectly well how it came into being and is aware of the tragedies which convinced its peoples of the need to unite, it is less clear about the direction it should take from here. Should it set itself up as a federation akin to the United States of America, inspired by a continent-wide patriotism which will transcend and absorb those of its constituent nations? Should it possess not only economic and diplomatic power on the world stage, but also political and military power? Would the EU be ready to take on such a role, and the responsibilities and sacrifices that go along with it? Or should it be content with being a flexible partnership between nations which jealously guard their own sovereignty and playing a supporting role as a global power?

For as long as the continent was divided into two rival camps, dilemmas such as these were irrelevant. Since then, they have become obsessive. Of course, there will be no return to the era of European wars and no new Iron Curtain. But it would be wrong to believe that these questions are just quarrels between politicians or among political scientists. The very destiny of the continent is at stake.

I shall come back to this question in more detail later, as I believe it is an essential one and not just for the people of Europe. I wanted to mention it here as an example of the loss of direction, the sense of disorientation and disorder which affects humanity as a whole and all of its constituent parts.

In truth, when I look at the various regions of the world, Europe worries me least, because it seems that more so than elsewhere it has taken stock of the scale of the challenges facing humanity; because it has the necessary people and institutions to debate them effectively and work out solutions; and because the EU provides a project to commit to and strong ethical concerns, even if sometimes it seems to take them too readily for granted.

Regrettably there is nothing comparable elsewhere. For decades the Arab-Muslim world had been sinking deeper and deeper into a historic pit from which it seemed incapable of extricating itself. It felt rage against the whole world – the West, the Russians, the Chinese, the Hindus, the Jews, and so on – and above all against itself. The countries of Sub-Saharan Africa, with rare exceptions, are plagued by civil wars, epidemics, sordid trafficking, widespread corruption, disintegrating institutions, a fraying social fabric, mass unemployment and despair. Russia is struggling to recover from seventy years of Communism and the chaotic way it ended; its leaders dream of regaining their former power, while its people remain disillusioned. The United States, meanwhile, having defeated its principal global adversary, finds itself engaged in a titanic enterprise which is wearing it down and leading it off course: trying to tame an untameable planet almost single-handed.

Even China, which has experienced a spectacular rise, has reason to be worried. For even if now, at the beginning of this century, its path seems clear – to relentlessly pursue economic development while carefully preserving its cohesion as a society and a nation – its future role as a political and military power is beset with serious uncertainties, as much for China itself as for its neighbours and the rest of the world. The Asian giant still possesses a more or less reliable compass, but it is getting close to a point where it will no longer be of use.

In one way or another, all the people on earth are in the same storm. Rich or poor, arrogant or downtrodden, occupiers or occupied, they are – *we* are – all aboard the same fragile raft and we are all going down together. Yet we go on insulting and quarrelling with each other, without heeding the rising tide.

We might even cheer if a devastating wave heading towards us engulfed our enemies first.

2

There is another reason why I chose the European Union as my first example: it provides a good demonstration of a phenomenon known both to historians and to each of us in our own lives – namely that failure may turn out to be providential and success may turn to disaster. The end of the Cold War seems to me to be a deceptive event of that sort.

The fact that Europe's triumph has caused it to lose its bearings is not the only paradox of our times. One could argue in the same way that the West's strategic victory, which should have consolidated its supremacy, has accelerated its decline; that the triumph of capitalism has precipitated the worst crisis in its history; that the end of the 'balance of terror' has created a world obsessed with 'terror'; and also that the defeat of a notoriously repressive and anti-democratic Soviet system has greatly diminished the quality of political debate all over the planet.

I want to focus on the last of these points first, to underline the fact that with the end of bipolar confrontation we went from a world in which divisions were mainly ideological and the debate incessant to a world in which the divisions are mainly on identity lines and leave little room for debate. Everyone asserts his own allegiances in front of others, utters his curses, mobilises his own people, demonises his enemies – for what else is there to say? Adversaries today scarcely speak the same language.

That is not to say that I miss the intellectual climate of the Cold War (which was not to begin with cold everywhere – it splintered into numerous side conflicts which cost millions of lives, from Korea to Afghanistan, Hungary to Indonesia, and Vietnam to Chile and Argentina). It seems to me nonetheless legitimate to deplore the fact that the world emerged from the Cold War at the lowest level, by which I mean heading towards *less* universalism, rationality and secularism; towards a reinforcement of inherited allegiances rather than acquired knowledge; and thus towards less open debate.

During the ideological confrontation between Marxism's supporters and its opponents, the whole planet resembled a huge amphitheatre. In newspapers, universities, offices, factories, cafés and homes, most human societies were buzzing with endless discussions of the pros and cons of this or that economic system, philosophy or way of organising society. Since the defeat of Communism, when it ceased to offer humanity a credible alternative, these exchanges have lacked a subject. That may be why so many people have turned their backs on their tattered utopias and sought shelter under the reassuring roof of their community. It may also be the case that the political and moral defeat of resolutely atheist Marxism has renewed enthusiasm for the beliefs and forms of solidarity which Marxism sought to root out.

The fact remains that, since the fall of the Berlin Wall, we find ourselves in a world in which allegiances – especially religious ones – are stronger; in which coexistence between different human communities is as a result a little more difficult each day; and in which democracy is constantly at the mercy of identity politics and one-upmanship.

This slide from ideology to identity has had devastating effects all across the globe, but nowhere more so than in the Arab-Muslim world, where religious radicalism, long the preoccupation of a persecuted minority, has achieved massive intellectual predominance within most societies as well as in the diaspora. In the course of its rise, this tendency began to adopt a violently anti-Western stance.

This development, set in motion by the advent of Ayatollah Khomeini in 1979, has become more pronounced since the end of the Cold War. As long as the confrontation between the two blocs lasted, most Islamist movements were markedly more hostile to communism than capitalism. They may never have had any sympathy with the West, its politics, way of life or values, but the Marxists' militant atheism provoked their hostility. At the same time, the Islamists' local enemies, especially the Arab nationalists and left-wing parties, followed the opposite path, becoming allies or clients of the Soviet Union. This alignment was to have disastrous consequences for them, but it was in a way dictated by their history.

For generations, the modernist elites of the Arab-Muslim world sought in vain to square the circle, that is to say, to Europeanise without giving in to the hegemony of the European powers which dominated countries from Java to

Morocco and which controlled their resources. Their independence struggles had, after all, been fought against the
British, French and Dutch, and each time their countries
tried to take control of key sectors of their economies, it was
Western oil companies – or in the case of Egypt, the Franco-
British Suez Canal Company – that they came into conflict
with. The emergence in Eastern Europe of a powerful bloc
which advocated rapid industrialisation, touted the slogan
'friendship between peoples', and firmly opposed the colonial powers struck many of them as a way out of this impasse.

In the aftermath of independence struggles, looking to the
Communist states seemed reasonable and promising. In
hindsight, it turned out to be disastrous. The elites of the
Arab-Muslim world didn't achieve development, national
liberation, democracy or social modernity; all they got was a
local, nationalistic brand of Stalinism entirely lacking the
attributes that had given the Soviet regime its international
influence: its internationalist rhetoric, its massive contribution to the defeat of Nazism from 1941 to 1945, and its
ability to build a military power of the first order. Instead, all
that the so-called 'progressive' Arab regimes were able to
imitate were the Soviet model's worst defects: its tendency
to xenophobia, police brutality, notoriously ineffective
economic planning, as well as the confiscation of power by
the party, a clan or the leader. Saddam Hussein's secular
regime was a telling example of this.

Deciding whether to blame the age-old blindness of Arab
societies or the age-old greed of Western powers matters
little today. Both positions can be defended and I shall return

to them. What is certain – and what weighs heavily on the world today – is that for several decades the secular, potentially modernising elements of the Arab-Muslim world fought *against* the West, and in so doing headed down a dead end materially and morally, and that the West fought back, often with devastating effectiveness, and sometimes with the support of Islamic religious movements.

This was not a true alliance, merely a tactical arrangement to confront a powerful common enemy. But it meant that at the end of the Cold War the Islamists were on the winning side. Their influence on daily life became visible and far-reaching in all areas. Now a large part of the population identified with them, all the more strongly as they adopted all the social and nationalist demands traditionally championed by the left and resistance movements. While it remained based on the clear application of the precepts of faith, often interpreted conservatively, Islamist discourse became politically radical: more egalitarian, more supportive of the Third World, more revolutionary and more nationalistic – and from the end of the twentieth century, resolutely hostile to the West and its protégés.

A comparison comes to mind in relation to this last point: in Europe, right-wing democrats and communists who had been allies against Nazism during the Second World War found themselves enemies in 1945. Likewise, it was predictable that at the end of the Cold War, the Islamists and the West would become implacable foes. If somewhere suitable for the touch paper to be lit was required, Afghanistan provided it. That was where these former allies were last united in battle against the Soviets; that was where, after their final victory in the last decade of the twentieth century, their breach became definitive; and it was from there that, on 11 September 2001, a deadly attack was launched against the US. The chain reaction which followed is well known – invasions, insurrections, executions, massacres, civil wars and countless further terrorist attacks.

3

The idea that the West is facing a handful of terrorists who take the name of Islam in vain and whose actions are condemned by the vast majority of believers doesn't always match reality. It is true that monstrous acts of carnage, such as the one perpetrated in Madrid in March 2004, arouse feelings of disgust, awkwardness and sincere condemnation in the Muslim world. But if you look closely at the different 'tribes' which make up humanity today across our planet, their reactions to terror attacks, like those to armed conflicts and political shows of strength, are rarely the same: what causes some people to feel outrage may be justified, excused or even applauded by others.

We are obviously in the presence of two interpretations of history, which crystallise around different perceptions of 'the enemy'. For some, Islam has shown itself incapable of adopting the universal values advocated by the West, while for others, the West above all possesses a will to universal domination, which Muslims have tried hard to resist with their limited remaining resources.

For someone able to listen to each 'tribe' in its own language, as I have done for many years, this spectacle is at once instructive, fascinating and depressing. For, as soon as you accept certain premises, everything can be interpreted coherently without needing to hear the other side's opinion.

If, for example, you accept the conjecture that the great calamity of our time is the 'barbarity of the Muslim world', looking at Iraq will only confirm your view. You will see a bloody tyrant whose reign of terror lasted a third of a century; who slaughtered his own people and squandered their oil wealth on luxuries and military spending; who invaded his neighbours, defied the great powers, became increasingly boastful, to the delight of the Arab masses, before folding without putting up a real fight. Then, after his fall, watch as the country sinks into chaos and see the different communities begin to massacre each other, as if to say: 'You see, it took a dictator to keep a people like this in line!'

If, on the other hand, you take the cynicism of the West for granted, events can be explained just as coherently: as a prelude there were sanctions, which plunged a whole nation into poverty and cost the lives of hundreds of thousands of children but didn't ever deprive the dictator of his cigars. Next came an invasion, justified on a false premise and carried out in contempt of public opinion as well as international institutions, and motivated at least in part by the desire to gain control of Iraq's oil resources. Then, following the US victory, there was the hasty and arbitrary dissolution of the Iraqi army and machinery of state, the explicit implantation of communitarianism within its institutions as if it had been decided to plunge the country deliberately into a state of permanent instability; and for good measure, the barbaric acts of Abu Ghraib prison, systematic torture, endless

humiliation, collateral damage, innumerable blunders that
have gone unpunished, looting, waste . . .

To some, the case of Iraq demonstrates that the Muslim
world is impervious to democracy. To others, it reveals the
true face of Western 'democratisation'. Even in the footage
of the death of Saddam Hussein, the ferocity of the Americans
is as evident as that of the Arabs.

In my view, both positions are correct and both are wrong.
Each follows its own orbit around its public, which grasps its
subtleties but doesn't hear the opposing side. As a result of
my background and the course my life has taken, I ought to
belong within each of these orbits at the same time, but I feel
myself growing daily more distant from them both.

This feeling of 'estrangement' is not due to some desire to
establish an equivalence of blame between these aspects of
my identity. Nor is it due simply to my irritation at two types
of cultural obstinacy which are poisoning the early years of
this century – and which, incidentally, are contributing to
destroying my native land. My criticism applies to the way
both the West and the Arab world have behaved for many
centuries and it even leads me to question their raison d'être.
The essence of my idea is that both have reached the limits
of what they could still achieve as separate civilisations; that
they are both morally bankrupt, as are all the individual civilisations that still divide humanity; and that the moment has
come to transcend them. Either we will find a way this
century to build a common civilisation with which everyone
can identify, bound together by the same universal values,
guided by a powerful faith in the human adventure and

enriched by all our cultural diversity, or else we will descend together into a common barbarism.

What I resented most about the Arab world was its lack of moral conscience, and what I resented most about the West was its propensity to turn its moral conscience into an instrument of domination. As a result, the West's moral credibility was in perpetual decline and the Arabs' moral credibility was practically non-existent.

Nonetheless, I don't put the crises of 'my' two civilisations on the same level. Compared to what it was a thousand years ago, or three hundred, or even fifty, the West has undeniably experienced great advances, which on some levels are still going on and even accelerating. Meanwhile, the Arab world was at its lowest ebb, a cause of shame to its sons, its friends and its history.

One highly revealing example has been – and, unfortunately, still is – its ability to manage coexistence among its various religions and ethnic components. When I was young, relations between diverse Middle Eastern communities were still, if not egalitarian and fraternal, at least civil and decent. Sunni and Shia Muslims sometimes regarded each other with distrust, but intermarriage was common and the daily tit-for-tat massacres, which the Iraqi tragedy has made commonplace, would have been unthinkable.

When it came to Christian minorities, their situation was never idyllic, but they generally managed to survive and prosper whatever the regime and even prosper. At no time since the birth of Islam have they felt themselves as marginalised, oppressed and even forced out as they do today in Iraq and some other countries. Having become strangers in their own land, despite living there for centuries and sometimes even millennia, several of these communities will disappear in the course of the next twenty years, without it causing much distress among their Muslim compatriots or their fellow Christians in the West.

As for the Jewish communities of the Arab world, their extinction is already a fait accompli. There remain only here and there a few stoical survivors whom the authorities and populace continually humiliate and persecute.

But, one might object, do Israel and the US not bear some responsibility for this state of affairs? Yes, probably, but that is a shabby excuse for the Arab world to fall back on. Let us return to the example of Iraq. I believe that the erratic behaviour of the American occupier has contributed to plunging the country into intercommunal violence. I am even ready to admit, even though such cynicism strikes me as monstrous, that a few sorcerer's apprentices in Washington and elsewhere may have benefited from this bloodbath. But when a Sunni militant gets behind the wheel of a truck packed with explosives and detonates it in a marketplace full of Shia families and this mass murder is called 'resistance', and its perpetrator a hero or martyr by certain fanatical clerics, there is no point in blaming others; it is the Muslim world itself which needs to examine its conscience. What struggle is it engaged in? What values is it defending? What meaning does it accord its beliefs?

The Prophet is reported to have said: 'The best of men is the one who is most useful to his fellow men.' It is a powerful motto which sought to provoke some soul-searching among individuals, leaders and peoples: what are we contributing to others and to ourselves? In what way are we 'useful' to our fellow men? Are we guided by something other than suicidal despair, which is the worst form of sacrilege?

4

The West, the other civilisation to which I belong, has a different predicament from that of the Arab world, since it remains the model or at least the principal point of reference for all of humanity. Yet it too finds itself in a historic impasse today which is affecting its behaviour and contributing to a disordered world.

If, at the beginning of this century, there is a nagging 'Eastern question' which doesn't always seem as though it is progressing towards resolution, there is also undeniably a 'Western question'. And if the tragedy of the Arabs is that they have lost their place among nations and feel unable to recover it, the tragedy of the West is to have assumed too large a global role, which it can no longer entirely fulfil but from which it cannot extricate itself.

It goes without saying that the West has given humanity more than any other civilisation. Since the Athenian miracle two and a half thousand years ago, and especially in the course of the last six hundred years, there is not a field of knowledge, creativity, production or social organisation which – for better or for worse – does not bear the stamp of Europe or its North American offshoot. Western science has become science *tout court*; Western medicine *is* medicine, just as Western philosophy is synonymous with philosophy. Its various doctrines, from the most liberating to the most totalitarian, have been recreated under distant skies. Even those who fight against Western dominance do so with physical and intellectual tools which the West invented and spread around the rest of the world.

With the end of the Cold War, Western hegemony seemed to have crossed a new threshold. Its economic, political and social systems had demonstrated their superiority and appeared to be on the point of encompassing the whole world. There was even some premature talk of 'the End of History', since the whole world was now going to melt peacefully into the mould of the victorious West.

But History is not the wise and biddable virgin of ideologues' dreams.

And so in the field of economics, the triumph of the Western model has led paradoxically to a weakening of the West.

Freed from the shackles of central planning, China and then India's economies rapidly took off; these were two peaceful revolutions which were brought about quietly by unassuming people, but they are in the process of permanently changing the balance of the world.

In 1978, two years after the death of Mao Zedong, power fell to Deng Xiaoping, a little 74-year-old man who had miraculously escaped the purges of the Cultural Revolution. He immediately ordered the distribution of previously collectivised land to some of the peasants and allowed them to sell a proportion of their harvest. The results were convincing: productivity increased two-, three- and in some cases fourfold. Going further, the Chinese leader decided that, rather than being told by the local authorities, the peasants could henceforth choose for themselves what to plant. Production increased again. And so it began. By small steps and without earth-shattering declarations or mass demonstrations, the old unproductive system was progressively dismantled, progressively and yet at the speed of light, probably through the multiplier effect resulting from the size of the country's population. For example, when the authorities lifted the ban on small family businesses in the countryside – such as grocers', stalls and repair shops – twenty-two million of them sprang up, employing thirty-five million people. When it comes to China, one constantly has the impression of turning the pages of a book of records: for example, the number of skyscrapers in Shanghai in 1988 was fifteen, but within twenty years it had risen to five thousand – more than New York and Los Angeles combined.

But there are phenomena which do not depend on a giant scale, and which may even be made more difficult by it, such as the growth in GDP, which has hovered around an average of 10 per cent for thirty years, enabling the Chinese economy to overtake successively those of France, the UK, and then Germany in the first decade of the twenty-first century.

In India, the dismantling of the planned economy took place just as calmly and with consequences that were equally astonishing. In July 1991, the Indian government had to face

a major financial crisis which threatened imminent bank-
ruptcy. In response, the finance minister Manmohan Singh
decided to relax some of the restrictions which hampered
business. Up to that point, the country had had extremely
restrictive laws which obliged businesses to obtain a permit
for every transaction: import permits, foreign exchange
permits, investment permits, permits to increase production,
and so on. As soon as the economy was freed from these
shackles, it took off.

What I have described in a few brief paragraphs constitutes a
huge and unexpected advance for the whole of humanity,
one of the most exciting in history. The two most populous
countries on the planet, accounting for half of what we used
to call the Third World, are beginning to emerge from
underdevelopment. Other countries in Asia and Latin
America seem to be following suit. The traditional division
of the world into the industrial North and the impoverished
South is gradually fading.

   In retrospect, the economic rise of these great Eastern
nations will probably appear the most spectacular consequence of the collapse of state socialism. Viewing it from the
perspective of humanity as a whole, one can only applaud.
Seen from a Western standpoint, the joy is mixed with
apprehension, for these new industrial giants are not only
business partners; they also represent formidable rivals and
potential enemies.

   We are no longer in the traditional scenario of the
South offering cheap but inefficient labour. If Chinese
and Indian workers are still less demanding and may

remain so in the foreseeable future, they are better and better qualified and highly motivated. Are they less inventive, as is often claimed in the West, sometimes with a heavy hint of cultural or ethnic prejudice? If that is still the case today, the situation is likely to change as the men and women of the South become more self-confident, freer and less hampered by social hierarchies and intellectual conformity. Within a generation or two they could go from imitation via adaptation to innovation. The histories of these great peoples reveal that they are capable of it: porcelain, gunpowder, paper, the rudder, the compass, vaccination and the concept of zero are all testament to that. What these Asian societies once lacked they have now acquired or are in the process of acquiring under Western guidance. Freed from the caprices of power and opposition to change, having suffered the defeats, humiliations and poverty of the past, they seem at last ready to face the future.

The West has won; it has imposed its model. But by its very victory, it has lost.

Perhaps it would be useful to distinguish here between the universal, diffuse and implicit West, which has invaded the souls of all the nations of the earth, and the particular, geographic, political, ethnic West of the white nations of Europe and North America. It is the latter which today finds itself at an impasse, not because its civilisation has been overtaken by others, but because it has been adopted by others, depriving it of what constituted its specificity and superiority up to now.

With hindsight, perhaps we shall say that the attraction exerted by the Soviet system on the countries of the South paradoxically delayed the decline of the West. As long as China, India and many other centrally planned economies of the Third World remained prisoners of an economic model that did not work, they did not represent a threat to the West's economic supremacy – they in fact thought that they were fighting against it. They had to free themselves from that illusion and resolutely follow the dynamic path of capitalism before beginning to challenge the 'white man's' supremacy in earnest.

The Western nations experienced a golden age without realising it when they were the only ones who possessed an economic system that worked. In the competitive global environment that they did all in their power to create, they now seem condemned to dismantle entire sectors of their economy – almost all of industrial manufacturing has gone, along with a growing part of the service sector.

The situation is particularly acute for Europe, which, to put it simply, is caught in the crossfire between Asia and the US, by which I mean between the commercial competition of the emerging nations and the strategic competition of the US, whose effects are felt in cutting-edge industries such as aeronautics and military technology. To that we can add the further considerable European handicap: its lack of control over its gas and oil supplies, most of which are concentrated in the Middle East and Russia.

Another important consequence of the economic take-off of the Asian giants is that now millions of people have access to a style of consumption from which they were previously excluded.

One can smile indulgently or become outraged at certain excesses, but no one can legitimately deny these people the right to own what people in rich nations have long owned – fridges, washing machines, dishwashers, and all the products that go with them; hot water to wash in, clean water to drink, plentiful food; also medical care, education, leisure time, travel, and so on.

Unless bloody and absurd tyrannies are established across the planet to return these nations to poverty and servitude, I do not see how they can be prevented from doing what for decades they have been encouraged to do: work harder, earn more, improve their lives, and consume more and more.

For several generations, including my own, and especially for those of us who were born in the countries of the South, the struggle against underdevelopment was the logical extension of the struggle for independence. Independence seemed the easier challenge; the hard battle against poverty, ignorance, incompetence, social apathy and epidemics seemed as though it would take centuries. That the most populous nations have been able to take off before our eyes represents a sort of miracle which never ceases to amaze me.

That said, I must add on a less subjective note that the dizzying growth of the middle classes in China, India, Russia and Brazil – and all over the planet – is a reality which the world as it currently works does not seem able to accommodate. If in the near future three or four billion human beings were to begin consuming per capita as much as Europeans or

Japanese by head of population – not to mention Americans
– it goes without saying that we would see the world go
even further off course, ecologically as well as economically.
I scarcely need add that I'm not talking about some distant
future but the immediate one, perhaps even the present. The
pressure on natural resources – especially oil, water, raw
materials, meat, fish, cereals, etc – and the struggles over the
regions where they are produced; the determination of those
who have them to hold on to them, and of those who do not
to acquire them; all this provides enough fuel for innumerable deadly conflicts.

There is no doubt that these tensions will be lessened in a
period of global economic recession in which we will
consume less, produce less and worry less about resources
running out. But that relative lull will be more than compen-
sated for by the tensions produced by the crisis itself. How
will nations respond if their hopes of economic development
are subject to a sudden brutal interruption? What social
upheavals, what ideological and political follies, what military campaigns would such frustrations lead to? The only
similar event to which we can compare this is the Great
Depression of 1929. That led to social cataclysm, to an
unleashing of fanaticisms, to local conflicts, and to a worldwide conflagration.

We can reasonably hope that the most extreme scenarios
will not be repeated. But there will inevitably be shocks and
upheavals from which humanity will emerge transformed;
no doubt battered, bruised and traumatised, but perhaps also
more mature, more adult and more conscious than before of
sharing a common adventure on its frail raft.

5

The reduction of the West's share of the world economy, which began towards the end of the Cold War, has been accompanied by serious consequences which even now are not yet fully measurable.

One of the most worrying is that Western powers, especially the United States, seemed tempted to preserve through military superiority what they could no longer preserve through economic superiority or moral authority.

This may be the most paradoxical and perverse consequence of the end of the Cold War: an event that was supposed to bring peace and reconciliation has in fact been followed by a whole sequence of conflicts, with America going from one war to another without pause as though that had become the method of governance for the world's only superpower rather than a last resort.

The deadly attacks of 11 September 2001 do not fully explain this tendency. They may have reinforced it and partially legitimised it, but by and large it was already under way.

In December 1989, six weeks after the fall of the Berlin Wall, the US intervened militarily in Panama against General

Noriega. This expedition resembled a police raid and served as a warning: no one should be under any illusion about who was in charge of the planet and who had simply to obey. In 1991 there followed the first Gulf War; in 1992–3 the ill-fated mission in Somalia; in 1994 the intervention in Haiti to install Jean-Bertrand Aristide in power; in 1995 the war in Bosnia; in December 1998 the massive bombing campaign in Iraq dubbed 'Operation Desert Fox'; in 1999 the Kosovo conflict; from 2001 the war in Afghanistan and from 2003 the second Gulf War; in 2004 another intervention in Haiti, this time to remove President Aristide. And that doesn't even include the punitive bombings or smaller-scale military actions in Colombia, Sudan, the Philippines, Pakistan and elsewhere.

In each of these cases, a clear-sighted observer might be able to detect some legitimate motives along with others which are mere pretexts. But the abundance of examples is in itself disconcerting, as if military intervention had become a method of planetary governance is how I referred to it. More than once since the beginning of this century, it has crossed my mind that the truth may be yet more sinister and that these operations were carried out to set an example, as when colonial powers in the past sought to instil fear in the hearts of their indigenous subjects to quash any desire to revolt.

Some of the most dubious military interventions will remain associated with George W. Bush, and it is in part because of the Iraq War that the US electorate voted Barack Obama and the Democrats into office. It remains to be seen how far the tendency towards interventionism is linked to one

administration's political choices, and to what extent it is
determined by America's position in the world: that of a
country whose economic power is inexorably slipping,
which is clearly living beyond its means and getting ever
deeper into debt, and yet which possesses indisputable military superiority. How could it resist the temptation to play
this trump card to compensate for its weakness in other areas?

Whatever its president's feelings or its political convictions, the US can no longer allow its grip on the world to
weaken, nor lose control of the resources such as oil which
are essential to its economy; nor can it allow unimpeded
freedom of movement to the forces which would harm it or
look on passively as rival powers emerge which could one
day challenge its supremacy. If America gave up its close and
energetic management of world affairs, it would probably be
sucked into a spiral of declining power and declining affluence.

That does not mean that systematic interventionism is the
right answer to check decline; in fact, to judge by the first
years of this century, it has speeded it up. But would an alternative policy have the opposite effect? It may be worth
trying, but when a power loses its grip, the spontaneous reaction of its enemies is to overwhelm it and attack it rather
than express gratitude. The West was much more respectful
of Brezhnev's USSR than Gorbachev's, which it humiliated,
plundered and dismantled, creating a deep feeling of resentment among the Russian people. And the leaders of the
Iranian revolution were pitiless with President Carter, as he
had had scruples about conducting an aggressive policy.

What this means is that the West's dilemma over its relations with the rest of the world would not be miraculously

resolved if Washington suddenly altered its behaviour on the international stage. But such a change of attitude on the part of the sole superpower might prove to be crucial if we still hope for an era of trust and solidarity among all nations.

Some analysts make a distinction between hard and soft power. By the latter they mean the various ways in which a state can exercise its authority without always having recourse to its armed forces. Stalin's inability to understand this sort of power led him to ask how many divisions the Pope possessed. Moreover, the day the Soviet Union collapsed, from a strictly military perspective it still had the means to annihilate its enemies. But victory and defeat are not decided by armoured divisions, megatonnage of bombs or number of missile nose-cones. Those things are just one factor among many, and while great quantities of deadly weapons are undoubtedly necessary to maintain a great power, they are by no means sufficient. In any confrontation between individuals, groups or states, numerous factors come into play which may be a matter of physical power, economic capacity or moral influence. In the case of the Soviet Union, it is clear that it was morally discredited and economically crippled, which made its formidable military might useless.

Conversely, at the end of the Cold War, the West possessed overwhelming superiority in all three domains at once: military, thanks in particular to American power; economic, as a result of the financial, industrial and technological predominance of both Europe and the US; and moral, by virtue of its model of society, which had just defeated its most dangerous rival, Communism. This threefold superiority should have allowed the West to govern the world with subtlety, sometimes using the carrot and sometimes the stick, firmly discouraging rebellious enemies but offering everyone else substantial advantages to allow them to escape underdevelopment and tyranny.

That being so, it seemed reasonable to predict that recourse to arms would be very much the exception after the fall of Communism, and that it would be enough for the West to highlight the superiority of its own economic system and model of society in order to preserve its supremacy. More or less the opposite has happened. The West's economic supremacy has been eroded by the rise of the Asian giants, not to mention Russia and Brazil, and recourse to arms has become commonplace.

The West's moral supremacy has also been eroded, which is paradoxical to say the least, given that the Western model has no competitor and the appeal of the European and American lifestyle is stronger than ever not only in Warsaw and Manila, but also in Tehran, Moscow, Cairo, Shanghai, Chennai, Havana and everywhere else. Yet there exists a real problem of trust between the centre and the periphery. It is a problem which is rooted in the unhealthy relationship that was established in previous centuries between the Western powers and the rest of the world, and which today contributes to making people unable to manage their diversity, formulate shared values or envisage a common future. And that makes them incapable of facing today's growing dangers.

6

Part of the reason why the West has been unable to take full advantage of its victory over Communism is that it has not managed to share its prosperity beyond its cultural borders.

For example, the spectacular effects of the European project, which enabled several countries in the south and then the east of the continent to catch up after centuries of being left behind, has never managed to cross the narrow Strait of Gibraltar and reach the other side of the Mediterranean. There today there exists a high wall which may be invisible but is none the less as real, cruel and dangerous as the one which used to divide Europe.

The millennial crisis in the Muslim world may be responsible in part; it may even be the most significant factor. But it is certainly not the only one. Because if you look at the New World – a vast territory where Islam has never taken root – you will see a similar phenomenon: the United States has been unable to extend its prosperity to its Mexican neighbour south of the Rio Grande, to the point that the Americans felt the need to build their own protective wall (a real one in this case), which has caused distrust and resentment throughout Latin America, a continent which is, of course, as Christian as Europe and North America.

This makes me think that the failings of the Muslim world, however real and tragic they may be, are not the whole story. The Western world has its own historical blind spots and moral failures. And it is often these blind spots and moral failures that have coloured the experience of subjugated peoples over the last few centuries. When the United States is mentioned in Chile or Nicaragua, or France in Algeria or Madagascar, or Great Britain in Iran, China or the Middle East, or Holland in Indonesia, the names that come to mind are not Benjamin Franklin, Condorcet, Hume and Erasmus.

The Western reaction to this issue today is often an impatient one along the lines of: 'Stop blaming us! Stop beating us up over this! Not all the world's troubles are the fault of colonialism.' This is an understandable reaction, and strikes a chord with many people who, like me, were born in countries of the South and get irritated when they hear their compatriots blaming the colonial period for all their woes. That period did undoubtedly cause lasting traumas, especially in Africa, but the period since independence has often proven to be yet more disastrous, and I for one have no time for the countless incompetent, corrupt or tyrannical leaders who are always quick to offer the convenient excuse of colonialism.

I believe that the period of the French mandate in my own country, Lebanon, which lasted from 1918 to 1943, and also the final phase of the Ottoman presence (1864–1914), were much less harmful than the various regimes which have succeeded them since independence. It may be politically

incorrect to set it down in black and white, but this is how I
read the facts. (A similar pattern can be seen in several other
countries, but out of tact I shall mention only my own.)

But if the excuse of colonialism is no longer acceptable to
justify the failure of leadership in the Third World, the issue
of the unhealthy relationship between the West and its
former colonies remains crucial. It can't be shrugged off with
a quip or an irritated grumble.

For my part, I remain convinced that Western civilisation
has contributed more than any other to the creation of
universal values, but it has proved unequal to the task of
transmitting them effectively. The whole of humanity is now
paying the price for this failure.

The easy explanation is that other peoples are not ready
for the transplant. This is a tenacious idea which gets passed
on unquestioningly from generation to generation and
century to century, so obvious does it seem. Its most recent
outing came with the war in Iraq. 'The Americans' mistake',
so it is alleged, 'was wanting to impose democracy on a
people who didn't want it.' The statement is uttered like a
judgement which admits of no appeal, and everyone gets
something out of it, both Washington's detractors and its
supporters: the former mock the folly of such an undertaking and the latter praise its naive nobility. Such is the
cunning of this received idea, which fits every shade of
opinion and intellectual fashion. To those who are respectful
of other peoples, it seems respectful; but those who are
contemptuous or even racist also have their prejudices
confirmed.

It is an assertion with the appearance of a realistic assessment; but from my point of view it is quite simply the
opposite of the truth. What really happened in Iraq is that
the US was unable to bring democracy to a people who
longed for it.

Every time the Iraqis have had the chance to vote, they
have flocked in their millions, even at the risk of their lives.
Is there any other people on earth who would have queued
outside polling stations in the certain knowledge that there
would be suicide and car bombs? These are the people who
we are told did not want democracy. This is repeated in the
papers and in debates on the radio and on TV, and almost no
one takes the time to examine it critically.

The other part of the assertion – that the US wanted to
impose democracy – strikes me as equally dubious. It is
possible to come up with more or less credible reasons that
may have influenced the US decision to invade the country
in 2003: the fight against terrorism and regimes suspected of
aiding terrorists; the fear of a 'rogue state' developing
weapons of mass destruction; the desire to get rid of a leader
who threatened the monarchies of the Gulf and worried
Israel; the wish to control the oil fields; and so on. Explanations
with psychoanalytic overtones have even been put forward:
for example, that President Bush wished to finish off the job
that his father had left incomplete. But no serious observer,
none of the witnesses or researchers who have combed
through the accounts of meetings at which the decision to go
to war was taken and who have produced a voluminous
literature in recent years, has reported a shred of evidence to

suggest that the real motive for the invasion was to install democracy in Iraq.

While it would be pointless to base a judgement on intent, it must be conceded that from the very first weeks of the occupation, the US authorities put in place a system of political representation based on religious or ethnic origin, which immediately triggered outbreaks of violence unprecedented in the country's history. From my own firsthand experience in Lebanon and elsewhere, I can attest to the fact that communitarianism never causes democracy to flourish, to put it mildly. Communitarianism is a negation of the very idea of citizenship, and a civilised political system cannot be built on such a foundation. For all that it is crucial to take account of the different constituents that make up a nation (in a way that is subtle, flexible and implicit, so that every citizen feels he or she is represented), it is nonetheless pernicious and even destructive to set up a quota system which divides the nation permanently into rival tribes.

That the great American democracy brought the Iraqi people this poisoned gift of sacrosanct communitarianism is a shame and an indignity. If it was done out of ignorance, it is distressing; if it was a cynical calculation, it is criminal.

It is true that before the invasion and throughout the conflict there was much talk of freedom and democracy. Such utterances have been a matter of course everywhere and always. Whatever the objectives of a military operation, it is preferable to say that it was undertaken for justice, progress or civilisation; for God and his prophets; for widows and orphans; and also, of course, for legitimate self-defence and out of a love of peace. No leader wants people to say that his real motives were vengeance, greed, fanaticism, intolerance, the will to dominate or the desire to silence his opponents. The role of propagandists is to conceal the real aims behind noble disguises, and the role of free citizens is to scrutinise their actions to strip away the lies that cloak them.

That said, in the wake of the attacks of 11 September 2001 there was undoubtedly in the United States a brief infatuation with spreading democracy. When the nationalities of the members of the suicide squad became known, some officials expressed the opinion that America would be safer if the Arab world were governed by democratic, modernising regimes, and that the country had been wrong until then to support obscurantists and autocrats whose only virtue had been their willingness to be aligned with Washington. Shouldn't these 'clients' have been required to share some of the values revered by their protector?

This infatuation – translated into high-flown slogans such as 'the Greater Middle East' or 'the New Middle East' – misfired. I shall not dwell therefore on this episode, but perhaps I may express *en passant* my astonishment at this spectacle: the leader of the Western democracies wondering at the dawn of the twenty-first century if it might not be a good idea after all to support the emergence of democratic regimes in Egypt, Arabia, Pakistan and the rest of the Muslim world. Having encouraged almost everywhere powers whose first virtue was 'stability' without looking too closely at how they maintained it; having supported ultra-conservative leaders without worrying about the ideology upon which

their conservatism was based; having trained highly repressive security and police forces, especially in Asia and Latin
America, now the great American democracy wondered if it
wouldn't be a good idea after all to play the democracy card.

But this fine idea was soon forgotten: after three laps of the
track, the land of Abraham Lincoln reached the conclusion
that all this was much too risky; that feelings were running so
high that free elections would bring the most radical elements
to power almost everywhere; and that it was better therefore
to stick to tried and tested solutions. Democracy would have
to wait.

7

In the months that led up to the invasion of Iraq, Secretary of State Colin Powell often found himself in the most awkward situation imaginable: having to convince the whole world that the war absolutely had to go ahead, while in private making great efforts to persuade his president not to proceed.

In a one-to-one meeting at the White House on 13 January 2003 he reportedly warned him: 'You break it, you own it.' It is a policy that some shops apply, according to which a customer who breaks an item has to pay for it. Powell spelled it out to the president in the following terms: 'You are going to be the proud owner of twenty-five million people. You will own all their hopes, aspirations, and problems. You'll own it all.'

Colin Powell's warning did not just hold good for those who were about to 'break' Iraq. In a single sentence, this son of Jamaican immigrants, who had become chief of the US armed forces and then in charge of its foreign policy, had defined the historical responsibility of victors and put his finger on the perennial problem of Western powers: as soon as they had established their hegemony over the whole planet, demolishing the political, social and cultural structures that used to prevail, they became moral guardians of the future of conquered peoples and should have thought seriously about the way in which they behaved towards them – whether they should welcome them in gradually like adopted children, applying the same laws to them as to Europeans, or simply tame them, subdue them and crush them.

A child can tell the difference between an adoptive mother and a stepmother. A people can tell the difference between liberators and occupiers.

Contrary to the received idea, the perennial fault of the European powers is not that they wanted to impose their values on the rest of the world, but precisely the opposite: it is that they have constantly renounced their own values in their dealings with the peoples they have dominated. As long as this misunderstanding remains, we will run the risk of falling into the same error again.

The first of these values is universality, the belief that humanity is one. Diverse, but one. That being so, it is an unforgivable error to compromise on fundamental principles on the perennial pretext that others are not ready to adopt them. There is not one set of human rights for Europe and another for Africa, Asia and the Muslim world. No people on earth is made for slavery, tyranny, arbitrary power, ignorance, obscurantism or the subjugation of women. Every time this fundamental truth is overlooked, we betray humanity and we betray ourselves.

★   ★   ★

I happened to be in Prague in December 1989, as the demonstrations against Ceausescu were beginning in Bucharest. Immediately there was a spontaneous expression of solidarity with the Romanian people in the Czech capital, which had recently been liberated in the 'Velvet Revolution'. On a sign near the cathedral someone had written in English: 'Ceausescu, you don't belong in Europe!' The anger of the anonymous sign-writer was understandable, but his way of expressing it shocked me. I wanted to ask him on what continent a dictator *would* belong.

Sadly, what this person naively expressed is a widely held view. A dictator who would not be tolerable in Europe becomes acceptable when he plies his trade on the other side of the Mediterranean. Does this constitute a mark of respect for others? Respect for dictators, certainly, and therefore contempt for the people who endure them and for the values that democracies are supposed to promote.

But, some people may reply, isn't that the only realistic attitude? I don't think so. Not only is it wrong; it does not even make for a good bargain. When the West compromises its moral credibility, it also compromises its position in the world and ultimately its security, stability and prosperity. The West used to believe it could do so with impunity; now we know that everything comes at a price and that even old debts fall due. The statute of limitations is an invention of lawmakers; in people's memories, it does not exist. Or to be more precise, people who come through and manage to escape poverty, abasement and marginalisation, end up forgiving, without always abandoning their fears; those who do not come through dwell on it for ever.

This leads me to pose the crucial question again: have the Western powers really tried to transplant their values in their former possessions? Unfortunately not. Whether in India, Algeria or elsewhere, they have never accepted that the indigenous peoples they govern should celebrate liberty, equality, democracy, the spirit of enterprise or the rule of law; indeed, they have even constantly repressed them whenever they have demanded these things.

So much so that the elites in colonised countries have had no choice but to seize those denied values themselves, against the wishes of their colonisers, and turn them on their colonisers.

A detailed, dispassionate reading of the colonial era shows that there have always been exceptional characters among the Europeans: administrators, soldiers, missionaries, intellectuals and some explorers such as Savorgnan de Brazza, whose behaviour was generous, equitable, sometimes even heroic, and certainly in keeping with the precepts of their faith and the ideals of their civilisation. The colonised sometimes remember such characters; that is probably why the Congolese retained the name of Brazzaville.

But they were the exceptions. As a general rule, the policy of the Western powers was mainly dictated by greedy companies and colonists who jealously guarded their privileges and feared nothing so much as the advancement of the 'natives'. When from time to time an administrator sent from

Europe advocated a different policy, they tried to influence him with bribes or intimidation. If he proved stubborn, arrangements were made to get him recalled. Once in a while, a civil servant deemed to be idealistic was mysteriously killed, as probably happened to Brazza . . .

It is often said that the West 'even' alienated the most modernist elites in the countries of the South. This statement is so incomplete as to be misleading. It seems to me that it would be more accurate to say that the West has alienated even the modernist elites, while it has constantly found accommodations, common ground and convergences of interests with regressive forces.

The West's tragedy, today as it has been for centuries, is that it is perpetually torn between its desire to civilise the world and the will to dominate it – two irreconcilable impulses. Everywhere it has enunciated the most noble principles but it has carefully refrained from applying them in its conquered territories.

This was not a trivial mismatch between political principles and their application on the ground; it was a systematic abandonment of the ideals that had been proclaimed, which as a result aroused the lasting mistrust of the elites in Asia, Africa, Arabia and Latin America, and especially among those who believed most wholeheartedly in Western values, who had adopted the principles of equality before the law, and freedom of speech and association. It was these modernist elites who formulated the boldest claims, finding themselves prey to inevitable disappointment and resentment, while traditionalist elements put up with colonial authoritarianism more easily.

This missed opportunity turns out today to have been very costly. Costly for the West, because it finds itself without its natural intermediaries in the countries of the South; costly for the peoples of the East, because they find themselves without their modernising minorities who could have constructed democratic free societies; and costly, above all, for those minorities themselves, those frontier people, those hybrid nations, for all those who in the countries of the South bear the mark of the West and also for those who emigrated to the North and bear the mark of the South, the very people who in better times could have played the role of go-betweens and who are now the first victims.

8

Anyone who detects in my words the anger of a member of a minority group from the Middle East would be only half wrong. I in fact belong to a species which is heading for extinction, and I will refuse to my dying breath to consider as normal the emergence of a world in which communities which have lasted for millennia, and which are guardians of the most ancient of human societies, are forced to pack up and abandon their ancestral homes to seek refuge in foreign lands.

It is natural that the victims should feel moved; it's worrying that they should be the only ones to feel moved. The problem of minorities is not just a problem for the members of those minorities. What is at stake is 'not simply' the fate of a few million people, so to speak. What is at stake is the raison d'être and purpose of our civilisation; if, at the end of a long process of material and moral evolution, it ends up with such ethnic and religious 'cleansing', this is a clear sign that it has taken a wrong turn.

For any society, just as for humanity as a whole, the fate of minorities is not just one issue among many; it is, along with the treatment of women, one of the surest indicators of moral progress, or decline. A world in which human diversity is respected a little more each day, in which everyone is able to speak the language he chooses, profess his beliefs peacefully and come to terms with his origins calmly without encountering hostility or denigration from the authorities or the population at large, is a world which is advancing, progressing, on the up. On the other hand, how can one not speak of decline in a world in which identities are suppressed, as is the case today in the vast majority of countries in both the northern and southern hemispheres, and in which it becomes more difficult each day to use one's own language or practise one's faith?

In 2007, I became particularly concerned about the dangers faced by the Mandaeans, a tiny community caught up in turmoil and threatened with imminent extinction. The Mandaeans, also known as the Sabaeans, are a community so small, discreet and unassuming that few people outside Iraq know of their existence.

I myself had not heard of them until 1988, when I was doing some research on Mani, the founder of Manichaeism, an astonishing character who lived in Mesopotamia in the third century CE. While looking for information on his youth and the origins of his doctrine, I discovered that he spent his earliest years with his father in an oasis on the banks of the Tigris, south of present-day Baghdad, in a gnostic community which venerated Saint John the Baptist and followed his example in practising baptism by immersion. I was then delighted to find out that this particular community, which one might have imagined had disappeared centuries ago, had in fact survived in more or less the same place and carried out the same sort of baptisms in the same river. By what miracle this came about I do not know. The explanation is to be found in part in the Qur'an, which accords special status to 'people of the Book', such as Jews, Christians and Zoroastrians, and also mentions the Sabaeans – in Arabic, *al-sabi'a*, a name which seems to derive from a Semitic root denoting the idea of immersion. Armed with this protection, the community somehow managed to survive the past fourteen centuries. It was never easy: existing on the margins of tolerance, they had always to be self-effacing, which nonetheless was not enough to protect them from periodic persecution and regular humiliation.

Throughout this whole period, the community simultaneously laid claim to the name Sabaeans, which reminded their Muslim neighbours of their mention in the Qur'an, and Mandaeans, which comes from another Semitic root meaning 'knowledge', the equivalent of *gnosis* in Greek. Under these twin names, they managed to maintain their faith and the coherence of their community; moreover, although they made a point of writing and speaking Arabic, they were able to preserve their own language, which linguists call Mandaic, a variant of Aramaic, which apparently even includes some terms derived from Sumerian. It is a language which, incidentally, possesses a little-known literature.

The fact that this last gnostic community has been able to survive until the present day has never ceased to fascinate and move me for the past twenty years. It is as if there were still a Cathar community in some inaccessible valley in the south of France which had miraculously survived the holy wars, as well as everyday persecutions, and still practised its rites in the langue d'Oc.

I didn't choose this example at random. When you look for the origins of Catharism and other movements inspired by Manichaeism which spread through Europe between the tenth and the thirteenth centuries, such as the Bogomils in Bulgaria and Bosnia, and the Patarenes of Italy, you find the original source in Mesopotamia in the third century, in that oasis by the Tigris where Mani's doctrine developed.

My anger on learning in early March 2007 that the Mandaeans were now threatened with extermination is not hard to imagine: they were suffering like all Iraqis from the bloody madness that had afflicted the country and, in the unprecedented outbreak of religious fanaticism, even their Qur'anic dispensation could no longer protect them. Zealous preachers now denied them the status that the Islamic holy book had clearly granted them. In Fallujah, terrified families had been forcibly converted at knife-point; in Baghdad and throughout the country, the Mandaeans had been chased from their jobs, expelled from their homes and had their shops looted. 'We have suffered a thousand trials,' one of their leaders wrote to me, 'but this one could prove fatal. We are threatened with imminent annihilation.' Their numbers, already low, had collapsed again: in 2002 there must have been around thirty thousand of them in the whole of Iraq; four years later only six thousand remained. Their community had been pursued and scattered, and was now in a state of disarray. They could no longer assemble or worship; they no longer even knew where to bury their dead.

Some people eventually rallied to their support, and a discreet operation was launched which enabled most families to find asylum, mainly in Sweden. But they have little chance of surviving as a community. In a few years their language will no longer be spoken, and their rituals will be reduced to a sham. A culture that lasted over a thousand years will have disappeared as we looked on indifferently.

My reason for mentioning the Mandaeans is that their tragedy seems revealing of how our civilisation has gone off course. The fact that such a community was able to survive so many centuries only to be extinguished before our eyes says much about the barbarism of our times, and in particular that of the two cultural spheres to which I belong, the Arab world and the West.

Today the Arabs seem unable to tolerate what they tolerated fifty, a hundred or even a thousand years ago. Books published in Cairo in the 1930s are banned today on the grounds of impiety; debates which took place in Baghdad in the ninth century in the presence of the Abbasid caliph on the nature of the Qur'an would be unthinkable today in any Muslim city, even in a university. To think that one of the greatest classical poets in the Arab language is universally known by the name Al-Mutanabbi, literally 'he who calls himself prophet', because in his youth he travelled through Iraq and Arabia making such claims! In his day in the tenth century, this provoked shrugs, frowns and jokes, but it never prevented believers from listening to the poet and admiring his talent; today, he would get himself lynched or decapitated without further ado.

In the West, barbarism does not take the form of intolerance or obscurantism, so much as arrogance and insensitivity.
The US army charges into ancient Mesopotamia like a
hippopotamus in a field of tulips. In the name of freedom,
democracy, self-defence and human rights, people have been
mistreated and killed, buildings demolished. Seven hundred
thousand deaths later come a withdrawal and muttered
excuses. Nearly a trillion dollars – and according to some
estimates two or three times as much – has been spent, but
the occupied country is poorer than before. The US wanted
to fight terrorism, but it is flourishing more than ever.
President Bush's Christian faith was pushed to the fore, and
now every church cross is suspected as a sign of collabora-
tion. They claimed they were establishing democracy, but
went about it in such a way that the very notion of democracy will remain discredited for a long time to come.

America will get over its Iraqi trauma. Iraq will not get over
its American trauma. Its largest communities will have
suffered hundreds of thousands of deaths; its smaller communities will never recover their place – not just the Mandaeans
or the Yazidis, but also the Assyro-Chaldaeans, whose very
name evokes marvellous episodes in our great human story.
Now the fate of all these minorities is sealed: at best, they
will end their progress through history in some faraway place
of exile; at worst, they will be annihilated on the spot,
crushed between the twin jaws of today's barbarism.

9

We contemplate earlier times with a condescension which, given our current behaviour, is unjustified. The century which recently ended certainly saw wonderful advances: many more of us live much longer and better; we have at our disposal tools and medicines which only a few centuries ago would have seemed to belong to the domain of science fiction if they were conceivable at all. But the same century also witnessed totalitarian regimes much more terrible than the tyrannies of earlier centuries and produced weapons which for the first time in history were capable of destroying all trace of civilisation on earth.

Does that mean that humanity progressed materially but not morally? That would not be quite true. We undeniably advanced in the course of the twentieth century on all fronts simultaneously, but not at the same speed. While in the acquisition of knowledge, in the development of science and its technological adaptation for civil and military ends, and in the production and distribution of wealth, change was rapid and upward, that of human behaviour was in the main inadequate, and tragically so.

Inadequate is the term which best describes our response

to our current predicament. The relevant question is not whether our attitudes and behaviour have progressed in comparison to those of our ancestors; it is whether they have changed *enough* to allow us to face the enormous challenges of the contemporary world.

One example among many is that of the environment, atmospheric pollution and climate change. There has been a remarkable realisation of the importance of this previously neglected field, probably less marked in some countries than in others, but real and even spectacular. In a few decades, effective measures have been taken and centuries-old habits have been changed. When one recalls that in London in early December 1952, smog (a mix of smoke and fog) caused the deaths of twelve thousand people in five days, one can see how far we have come. In most industrialised nations, the authorities have taken steps to make factories less polluting and have banned the construction of new ones near large population centres. This is a healthy practice which has spread since the end of the Cold War to the countries of the former Eastern bloc, which previously had a dreadful track record in this regard.

This is progress we can be pleased about, but it is not enough to sweep away our current fears. Since the planet is suffering a warming that is speeding up as a result of our carbon emissions and could prove disastrous for future generations, it isn't enough to ask ourselves, 'Is our behaviour in this area better than that of our parents and grandparents?' The answer to that question is undoubtedly yes. The relevant question is: 'Will our behaviour in this area allow us to avoid the deadly threat which hangs over our children and grandchildren?'

It goes without saying that a positive answer to the first question would offer no reassurance if the answer to the second question turns out to be no. As I write, this cannot be ruled out. For if we want to reduce the carbon emissions in the atmosphere significantly, the world's richest and most powerful people, notably those in America, Europe and Japan, would have to accept profound changes in their consumption habits; equally, the major nations of the South, whose economic take-off has only just begun, would have to agree to limit their growth.

In order to be able to impose such restrictive measures, which would demand serious sacrifices from every nation and every individual, there would have to be a major global step-change. There are no signs that this is imminent.

A similar discrepancy is apparent when it comes to the challenges posed by human diversity.

Today, with every culture daily confronting others and every identity experiencing the need for virulent self-affirmation, and every country and city having to organise a delicate coexistence, the question is not whether our religious, ethnic and cultural prejudices are stronger or weaker than those of previous generations; it is whether we will be capable of stopping our societies from drifting towards violence, fanaticism and chaos.

That is the situation in numerous regions of the world. The case of minorities in Iraq and the Middle East is not unique, though it has offered the most telling example in the first years of this century. If we turn out to be unable to ensure the survival of communities that have existed for centuries, the way we handle human diversity will have been proven deficient and inadequate.

That does not mean that in the past we were wiser, more attentive, tolerant, magnanimous or adept. A glance at a few history books is enough to show that there have always been bloodthirsty rulers, greedy despots, devastating invasions, pogroms, massacres and monstrous attempts at extermination. If some communities nonetheless survived century after century, it was because their fate was mainly linked to local vicissitudes and was not constantly affected by all the events on the planet.

When a serious incident took place in a village, it often took weeks for the rest of the country to hear of it, which limited its repercussions. Today the opposite is true: a clumsy pronouncement made at noon can serve as the pretext for slaughter that same evening ten thousand kilometres away. Sometimes it is a false rumour spread maliciously or through a misunderstanding which sparks violence. By the time the truth comes out, it is already too late: the bodies are piled up in the streets. I have in mind specific events that took place in the past few years, not just in Iraq but also in Indonesia, Egypt, Lebanon, India, Nigeria, Rwanda and the former Yugoslavia.

Some people may object that this is just a normal consequence of the evolution of the world. To which I would say, yes and no. The entanglement of men and conflicts is indeed natural a consequence of progress in communications. But what we have the right to deplore and denounce is that this technological advance has not been accompanied by an awareness that permits the preservation of peoples pitched against their will into the maelstrom of history.

What is at issue is the gulf that is opening up between our rapid material evolution, which brings us closer together every day, and our too slow moral evolution, which does not allow us to face the tragic consequences of our shrinking world. Of course, material progress cannot and should not be slowed. It is our moral evolution which must be considerably speeded up. It urgently needs to be raised to the level of our technological evolution, which demands a real revolution in attitudes.

I shall return later at greater length to the question of how we manage diversity as well as to climate change and our dilemmas in this crucial area. Here, I would like to focus for a moment on the turbulence in the economic and financial sector, in which we can see the same disparity between the scale of the problems which assail us and our feeble ability to resolve them.

Here, too, if it were a question of working out whether we will be able to act and think together better than in the past to mobilise emergency funds, the answer would certainly be yes. As soon as a crisis occurs, measures are taken, and although one could question their effectiveness and direction, they often enable some semblance of order to be restored.

But however much faith we place in leaders who meet in groups of two, seven, eight or twenty, with their hosts of competent advisers and reassuring press conferences, we still have to admit that every shock to the system is generally followed by another, more serious one. And this gives the impression that the previous response must have been inadequate.

After a certain number of slumps, one comes to the inevitable conclusion that this disparity is due not to misjudgements, but to the fact that the global economic system is more and more impervious to control. This is a failing which cannot be ascribed to a single cause, but it is certainly in part explained by a characteristic of our time which can be seen in numerous other fields: the fact that problems can only be solved by thinking globally, as though the world were a single, plural nation, whereas our political, legal and mental structures constrain us to think and act according to our specific interests – those of our states, electorate, businesses and national finances. Every government is inclined to think that what is good for it is good for everyone else. And, even if it is sufficiently clear-sighted to realise that this is not always the case, and even if some of its policies – protectionism, quantitative easing, discriminatory legislation and currency manipulation – have a negative impact on the rest of the world, it will nonetheless suit itself in its attempts to escape from stagnation. The only limit on the sacrosanct selfishness of nations is the necessity to avoid the collapse of the whole system.

This is a new kind of balance of terror which has been established, notably between the Chinese and the Americans – 'If you try to ruin me, I'll drag you down with me.' It is a risky game that leaves the planet at the mercy of a slip-up, and is no substitute for true solidarity.

★   ★   ★

Equally worrying is the fact that the economic turbulence that we see today has its origin in multiple types of disorder which affect the world and which come from both inside and outside the financial sector. Thus there are – alongside the data which allow the prediction that one year will see an economic slowdown and the next an upturn – many other factors whose effects cannot be reasonably predicted.

For example, extreme fluctuations in oil prices are due in part to speculation, but they are also influenced by the growing needs of the great nations of the South, and by political uncertainty in regions where oil is produced and across which it is transported – such as the Middle East, Nigeria, the Sahara, the Black Sea and the former Soviet Union – as well as several other factors. In order to control these fluctuations and prevent them from destabilising the wider economy, measures would probably have to be taken to discourage speculation at a global level. But there would also have to be concerted and equitable management of the planet's resources, changes in production and consumption methods, an end to the after-effects of the Cold War in improved relations between Russia and the West, and solutions found to a range of regional conflicts. That gives some indication of the scale of the problem, which demands a high degree of active solidarity between nations and which would take decades to achieve. Meanwhile the turbulence is affecting us today.

As soon as a government tries to tackle a problem, it finds that this problem is linked to a hundred others which belong to different areas and escape its influence. Whether it is fighting against recession, inflation and unemployment, or pollution, drugs, pandemics or urban violence, it inevitably

comes up against problems of all sorts – geopolitical, socio-
logical, sanitary, cultural or moral – which originate in all
corners of the planet; problems which absolutely have to be
solved if it is to have any chance of success, but on which it
can get little or no purchase.

In economics it has long been acknowledged as a matter of
common sense that if everyone acts according to his own
interests, the sum of those actions will be beneficial to the
general good. Selfishness would thus be paradoxically the truest
form of altruism. According to Adam Smith, every individual
'by pursuing his own interest . . . frequently provokes that of
the society more effectually then when he really intends to
promote it.' Writing in the eighteenth century, he also talked
of an 'invisible hand' which would providentially harmonise
the economic machine without the need for any authority to
intervene. It is a highly controversial vision, of course, but
not one that can be easily dismissed, given that it is at the
heart of the most successful economic system in human history.

What we do not yet know is whether this 'invisible' hand
is still capable of operating today, if it is able to 'lubricate' a
global market economy, combining societies with different
laws and innumerable individuals worldwide acting in unfore-
seeable ways as it used to be able to do for a few countries in
the West. It is probable in any case that no invisible hand
could prevent the growing wealth of nations weighing heavily
on the resources of the planet or polluting the atmosphere,
but neither is it certain that the visible hands of our leaders are
any better equipped to manage our global realities.

★   ★   ★

In the space of a few years we have seen two opposing belief systems thoroughly discredited. First, state power was stigmatised. In the wake of the failure of the Soviet system, all forms of planned economy seemed like heresy, even to some socialists. The laws of the market were deemed to be wiser, more effective and more rational. Almost everything was reckoned to be ripe for privatisation: health care, pensions, prisons and even, for the neo-conservatives in the White House, defence. The idea that the state had a duty to assure the well-being of its citizens was challenged, often implicitly, but sometimes explicitly. The principle of equality even came to be considered obsolete, a relic of a bygone age. There was felt to be no reason to be ashamed of flaunting disparities in wealth.

But the pendulum had swung too far and struck the wall, which sent it back in the opposite direction. Now belief in the infallibility of the market has been stigmatised. The virtues of the role of the state have been rediscovered. There have even been massive nationalisations, despite some distaste at using that word. Certainties which have been constantly trumpeted for three decades have been shaken and a radical reappraisal is under way, which will affect the political, social and economic spheres and will probably go far beyond that. How can a major financial crisis be resolved without attacking the crisis of confidence that accompanies it, the distortion in the scale of values, the loss of moral credibility of leaders, states, companies, institutions and those who are supposed to regulate them?

One of the most striking images from the first decade of this century was of Alan Greenspan, former director of the

Federal Reserve Board, testifying to a congressional
committee in October 2008. Though he denied that the
decisions he had taken, or failed to take, in the course of his
eighteen-year reign could have been responsible for the
cataclysm in the US sub-prime market and the ensuing
global turbulence, he admitted that he was in a state of
'shocked disbelief'. He was convinced, he said, that lenders
would never act in a manner which would compromise the
interests of their own shareholders. 'This modern risk-
management paradigm held sway for decades. The whole
intellectual edifice, however, collapsed in the summer of last
year.'

I suppose that those who doubt the inherent wisdom of
the mechanisms of the market will have responded to these
words with sarcasm. But what Greenspan expressed was not
just the disappointment of a misguided conservative. If his
remorse strikes me as significant, even touching, it is because
it marks the end of a period in which the behaviour of
economic agents had coherence and decency and obeyed
certain rules; in which big-spending, predatory and fraudu-
lent leaders were rare; and in which one could depend on
certain values and instantly recognise healthy businesses.

Without seeing earlier times – which had their share of
malpractice and crises – through rose-tinted spectacles, it has
to be admitted that there has never been a period quite like
our own in which those who are responsible for national
economies can no longer follow the acrobatic manipulations
of the financial whizz kids, and in which operators who
handle billions have no knowledge of political economy or
the least concern about the repercussions of their actions on

businesses, workers, or their own relatives and friends, without even mentioning the collective good.

It is easy to understand how old sages might become disenchanted. Whether they incline towards interventionism or laissez-faire, the doctors of the economy report disappointing results for their tried and tested therapies, as though they found themselves in front of a different patient from the one they treated the day before.

But this economic malaise may be just one aspect of a bigger, more complex phenomenon that affects all human societies without exception, rich or poor, weak or powerful, a phenom- enon we still refer to as the 'acceleration of history' but which goes far beyond what that meant last century. Perhaps it would be preferable to use another concept which better reflects the pace of change today: *instantaneity*. For, as so many examples show us every day, all world events now unfold in real time before the eyes of the whole of humanity.

It is no longer simply a matter of the pattern that has been imprinted on history for a long time – the accelerating move- ment of peoples, goods, images and ideas creating the impression of a shrinking world. We have got used to that over time. But the tendency became considerably more pronounced in the final years of the twentieth century, to the extent that one could say the phenomenon had changed its nature with the take-off of the internet, the ubiquity of email and the construction of the worldwide web, as with the development of some other means of instant communi- cation such as the mobile phone, which established instant links between people wherever they were, abolishing distance, reducing reaction times to nothing, amplifying the impact of events; and as a result increasing the speed at which they unfold.

That probably explains how the considerable upheavals, which in other centuries would have taken decades to unfold, now happen in the space of a few years or even months – for both better and worse. The first example that comes to mind is the uprooting in the space of a few years of cultures which had survived for millennia; but one could also think of the collapse of the Soviet Union, the expansion of the European Union, the growth of India and China, the rise of Barack Obama and a thousand other dramatic events.

Clearly the twenty-first century has begun in a mental atmosphere perceptibly different from any that humanity has known previously. It is a fascinating but dangerous change. To anyone interested in progress, the web today opens limitless perspectives: instead of just reading your local daily paper, you can look at the whole world's press while drinking your morning coffee at home, and especially if you read English, given that innumerable papers – in Germany, Japan, China, Turkey, Israel, Iran, Kuwait, Russia, etc – now publish an online edition in that language. For my part, I could lose myself in them for days on end without getting tired, in a state of amazement and the feeling of fulfilling a dream.

In Lebanon in my childhood I used to read all of the local press every morning. My father was editor of a daily paper and out of courtesy would send a copy of it to his colleagues on other papers, who would reciprocate by sending him theirs. 'Which one should I believe?' I asked him one day, pointing at the pile. Without interrupting his reading, he answered, 'None of them and all of them. None of them will tell you the whole truth, but each of them will give you its own version of it. If you read them all, and are able to exercise discrimination, you'll understand the essential.' My father did the same thing with radio stations: first the BBC, then Lebanese radio, then Cairo, followed by the Arabic-language broadcasts from Israeli radio; sometimes also Radio Damascus, Voice of America, Radio Amman or Radio Baghdad. By the time he had drained his coffee pot, he felt sufficiently well informed.

Often I think of the joy he would have felt if he could have experienced our era. There is no need to be the editor of a newspaper to receive all your country's media and that of the whole world at home, much of it free of charge. Anyone who wants to have a relevant, balanced, all-embracing view of what is really going on in the world has all they need at their fingertips.

But not everyone makes such use of the tools at their disposal. Not everyone wants to form a considered opinion. It is often the obstacle of language which prevents them from broadening the range of voices they listen to. But there is also an attitude of mind which is very common in all nations, which means that only a small minority feels the desire to hear what others are saying; many people make do with the version that flatters their own views.

For every person who navigates from one cultural universe to another with their eyes wide open, for every person who goes happily from the Al-Jazeera site to that of Haaretz, and

from the *Washington Post* to the Iranian press agency, there
are thousands who only visit their compatriots and fellow
believers, who imbibe only from familiar sources, who only
want to confirm their certainties and justify their resentments
in front of their screens.

So much so that this amazing modern tool, which ought
to encourage harmonious mixing and exchange between
cultures, becomes instead a rallying and mobilisation point
for the world's tribes. Not by dint of some conspiracy, but
because the internet, which accelerates and amplifies effects,
took off at a moment in history when identities were being
unleashed, the clash of civilisations was being established and
universalism was crumbling, the nature of debates was
becoming corrupted, violence was taking precedence in
words and deeds, and common reference points were
becoming lost.

It is not without significance in this context that this major
technological advance, which radically changed relations
between people, coincided with a strategic disaster of the
first order, namely the end of the confrontation between the
two great planetary blocs, the disintegration of the Soviet
Union and the socialist camp, the emergence of a world in
which differences of identity have taken over from ideological differences, and the advent of a single superpower which
unwillingly exerts de facto hegemony the length and breadth
of the planet.

I sometimes reread a dense little text published in 1973 by
the British historian Arnold Toynbee shortly before his
death. Surveying the trajectory of humanity, to which he

had devoted a magisterial study in twelve fat volumes, *A Study of History*, he distinguished three phases.

In the course of the first phase, which corresponds more or less to prehistory, people's lives were the same because 'however slow communication was, the pace of change was even slower'. Every innovation had time to spread to all societies before another came along.

During the second phase, which according to Toynbee lasted around four and a half millennia from the end of prehistory to about 1500 CE, change became more rapid than the speed of transmission, with the result that human societies became markedly different. It was during this phase that distinct religions, ethnicities and civilisations came into being.

Finally, from the sixteenth century, 'because the speed of change has been outstripped by the acceleration of the speed of communication', our habitat has begun to unify, at least technologically and economically, 'but not yet on the public level,' Toynbee observed.

This approach has the same value as all theories: each term, when examined closely, can give rise to criticisms, but the vision as a whole is thought-provoking. Especially when considered in the light of the last few decades. The acceleration has been dizzying, brutal and inevitably traumatic. Societies which had followed different courses throughout their histories, which had developed their beliefs, languages, traditions, feelings of belonging, their own sense of pride, found themselves catapulted into a world in which their autonomous identity was jostled, eroded and seemed under threat.

Their reaction has sometimes been violent and disordered, like that of a drowning person whose head is already under water and who struggles without hope or discrimination, ready to drag down with him anyone his hands grab hold of, whether would-be rescuers or aggressors.

From the end of the Cold War to the end of the 1980s, the evolution described by Toynbee towards an integrated civilisation progressed at a quite different pace and in an appreciably transformed strategic environment.

One government, that of the United States, found itself taking on the role of de facto global authority; its value system became the universal norm, its army the planet's police force, its allies vassals and its enemies outlaws. It is a situation without historical precedent. Certainly in the past there have been powers which at their height achieved some sort of primacy; which, like the Roman Empire, dominated the known world or extended so far that it was said the sun never set on their territories, such as the Spanish empire in the sixteenth century or the British empire in the nineteenth. But none of them possessed the technical means which would have allowed them to intervene at will all across the globe or to thwart the emergence of rival powers.

This process, which might have stretched out over several generations, was astonishingly accomplished in the space of a few short years. The whole world is now a unified political space. Toynbee's third phase has come to an abrupt, premature end and a fourth has begun which looks set to be stormy, troubling and eminently dangerous.

All of a sudden, the question of power and legitimacy has arisen at global level for the first time in history. If this essential fact is rarely expressly mentioned, it is constantly present in what is not said, in recriminations and at the heart of the most brutal conflicts.

In order for different peoples to accept the authority of a sort of global government, that government has to possess a legitimacy in their eyes other than that which stems from its economic and military power. And in order for individual identities to become part of a much larger identity and for particular civilisations to integrate into a planetary civilisation, it is imperative that the process take place in a context of equality, or at the very least of mutual respect and shared dignity.

I deliberately mixed different aspects in my previous sentences. The reality of today's world is only comprehensible if all these facets are constantly borne in mind. From the moment at which one civilisation predominates, carried by a single global superpower, transcending civilisations and nations can no longer happen in an atmosphere of serenity when a single civilisation prevails, led by a single global superpower. Peoples who feel themselves threatened with cultural annihilation or political marginalisation inevitably listen to those who call for resistance and violent action.

Unless and until the United States persuades the rest of the world that its pre-eminence possesses moral legitimacy, humanity will remain under siege.

II

Lost Legitimacy

I

As I write, an image comes into my mind which is trivial yet unforgettable: that of a polling station in Florida during the US presidential election in November 2000. A scrutineer is holding a ballot paper up to the light to work out from the perforations and twists in the paper whether Al Gore or George W. Bush should receive the vote.

Like millions across the world, I was hanging on the result of this count and the legal quarrel that accompanied it. In part, I admit, it was out of curiosity at watching an exciting political soap opera, but mainly it was because my own future and that of my nation were at stake in these elections. Back then I had an inkling of it, and today I am certain: that vote in Florida was to change the course of history in my native land, Lebanon.

I chose this spontaneously as my first example, as it closely affected me. I could have begun with many other more prominent examples, whose implications for the whole planet seem more obvious. For example, it is reasonable to suppose that the attacks on 11 September 2001 would still have taken place if Al Gore had been in the White House rather than George W. Bush. But it is also reasonable to suppose that

Washington's reaction would not have been the same. There would inevitably have been a 'war on terror', but with different priorities and slogans, and different methods and alliances. There would probably have been less determination, but also fewer mistakes. The president would not have spoken of a 'crusade' nor an 'axis of evil', and prisoners would not have been detained in Guantanamo. The war in Iraq would probably not have taken place. That would have made life very different for the people now caught up in it, as well as for US relations with the rest of the world. It is also probable that the Syrian army would not have had to leave Lebanon in 2005 and that the confrontations taking place in my country would have taken a different turn.

If the Democrats had won in November 2000, several other important issues might also have been handled differently – climate change, for example, or stem-cell research, or the role of the United Nations. This would have had significant consequences for the future of the planet. But it would be risky to take these hypotheses much further, and pointless to try to determine whether the world would now be in a better or worse state. I have pondered that famous vote in Florida over the years, and sometimes come to the conclusion it was disastrous and sometimes that it was providential.

In any case, one thing is certain: what the voters in Tampa and Miami were voting on in that symbolically significant first year of the new millennium was not just the future of the American nation; it was in large measure the future of every other nation as well.

The same thing could also be said of the next two presidential elections, in the course of which we experienced extreme situations. In 2004, the whole world wanted President Bush to be beaten, but his fellow citizens chose to re-elect him; the disaffection between America and the rest of the world was then at its height. Conversely, in 2008, all the nations on earth were in love with Senator Obama and when the vote went in his favour there was a torrent of admiration – entirely justified in my view – for the United States, its people, their political system and their ability to manage ethnic diversity. Such a convergence of opinion – linked to Obama's rhetoric, his African origins and the world being tired of the Republican administration – will not recur any time soon. On the other hand, it is highly likely that every US election henceforth will give rise to a global psychodrama.

That clearly poses a problem. I would even go as far as to say that beneath the anodyne, trivial exterior, the repercussions of US presidential contests are one of the hidden aspects of the political and moral disorder which characterises our times.

Before going any further, I should take account of two objections to which these thoughts could give rise. It is true, one could argue, that the US president is powerful today. His political decisions affect the fate of the whole planet, and therefore those who elect him find themselves in a role which is not theirs by right, since the choices they make so often prove decisive for the future of the peoples of Asia, Europe, Africa and Latin America. In an ideal world, it should not be thus. But why get worked up over a problem without a solution? After all, the people of Colombia,

Ukraine, China and Iraq can't be granted the right to vote in
US presidential elections.

I agree that would be absurd and it is certainly not what I
would advocate. What other solution is there? At this
moment, I can see none. But the fact that there is no realistic
solution does not mean that the problem does not exist. I am
convinced that it is entirely real and is already having devastating effects, and that its seriousness will become more and
more apparent in the coming decades.

I shall explain my reasons for these concerns in what
follows. First I would like to deal with another possible
objection. If the first was the perennial 'What's the point?',
the second is the no less enduring 'It has always been thus!'

Since the dawn of history, it will be objected, some nations
have imposed their will on others: the powerful decide; the
oppressed submit. For generations, the vote of someone in
New York, Paris or London has counted for more than that
of a voter in Beirut, La Paz, Manila or Kampala. If the present
day has brought changes, they have tended to be in a positive
direction, since hundreds of millions of people who have
previously been muzzled can now express themselves freely;
this is notably the case throughout most of Latin America
and Eastern Europe, and in some African and Asian countries
such as the Philippines and Indonesia.

That may be so, but it is deceptive nonetheless. Past
empires may have been vast and powerful, but their grip on
the world remained weak because their weapons and means
of communication did not allow them to maintain effective
control far from the centre, and also because they all had to
contend with rival powers.

Today, extraordinary technological advances have made possible much tighter control of the globe and contributed to the concentration of political power in a small number of capitals, and in one in particular. This explains the emergence for the first time in history of a government whose 'jurisdiction' covers the whole planet.

This unprecedented situation naturally generates equally unprecedented disparities as well as new balances – or rather imbalances. And suicidal resentment.

Clearly something has changed radically in the fabric of the world, something that has profoundly damaged relations between people, diminished the significance of democracy and blurred the path of progress.

If we want to examine this change more closely to try to understand its origins and mechanisms and to grope our way out of the deadly labyrinth, the concept which might serve as a beacon is that of legitimacy. In some people's eyes today, it is a concept which is outdated, forgotten and even somewhat suspect, but it is indispensable to any discussion of the question of power.

2

Legitimacy is what enables people to accept, without exces-
sive constraint, the authority of an institution, represented by
individuals and embodying shared values.

That is a broad definition capable of embracing very
different situations: a child's relationship with its parents, an
activist's with the leaders of his party or his union, a citizen's
with his government, an employee or a shareholder's with
the directors of a company, a student's with his professors, a
believer's with the leaders of his religious community, and so
on. Some forms of legitimacy are more stable than others,
but none of them is immutable; legitimacy can be won and
lost according to one's talent or to circumstances.

The whole history of human societies can even be told
from the viewpoint of crises in legitimacy. Following
dramatic change, a new source of legitimacy emerges which
replaces the one that has just collapsed. But how long that
new legitimacy lasts depends upon its successes. If it disap-
points, it will begin to fail fairly quickly, sometimes even
before its supporters realise it.

For example, at what point did the tsars stop appearing
legitimate? And how many decades did it take for the credit

of the October Revolution to run out in its turn? In recent times, Russia has been the scene of a spectacular loss of legitimacy which has had worldwide repercussions. But it is just one case among many. Legitimacy only *appears* unchanging; whether it belongs to a man, a dynasty, a revolution or a national movement, there comes a point at which it no longer works. It is at that point that one power replaces another, and a new legitimacy replaces the discredited one.

For the world to function reasonably harmoniously and without major disturbances, most people should have legitimate leaders in charge; they in turn would be answerable to a global authority which is itself regarded as legitimate.

Clearly that is not the case today. In fact it is almost the opposite: many of our fellow human beings live in states whose rulers are not the winners in fair elections, nor inheritors of a respected dynasty, nor continuing a successful revolution, nor architects of an economic miracle, and therefore do not have any legitimacy. And they live under the control of a global power whose legitimacy people do not recognise either. This is particularly the case for the vast majority of Arab nations. Is it a coincidence that this is where the men who committed the most spectacular acts of violence at the start of this century came from?

Questions of legitimacy have always played a major part in the history of the Muslim world. The most significant example is probably that of religious factionalism. While in Christianity there have been constant divisions – and sometimes massacres – over the nature of Christ, the Trinity, the Immaculate Conception and the form of prayers, the

conflicts in Islam have usually centred on quarrels over
succession.

The major schism between Sunnis and Shi'ites did not
come about for theological reasons but for dynastic ones. At
the death of the Prophet, a group of the faithful declared their
support for his young cousin and son-in-law, Ali. Ali possessed
a brilliant mind and had many unconditional supporters who
were called 'shi-'a-Ali', the party of Ali, or simply 'shi'a'. But
he also had many critics, who succeeded on three occasions in
having representatives from the opposing party named 'caliph'
or 'successor'. When Ali was finally chosen as the fourth
caliph, his enemies rose against him immediately and he was
never able to reign peacefully. He was assassinated four and a
half years later. Then his son Hussein was killed at the battle
of Karbala in 680 CE, an event still commemorated with great
fervour by Shi'ites. Many of them hope that a descendant of
Ali will soon appear among them: an imam hidden from us
today who will return power to its rightful owners. This
belief is held with a messianic zeal which the passing centuries
have not diminished.

Onto this dynastic quarrel have been grafted – as was the
case with the theological quarrels of Christians – considerations of a different order. When Rome condemned as heresy
the beliefs of the patriarch in Alexandria or Constantinople,
when Henry VIII of England broke with the Catholic
Church or a German prince supported Luther, there were
often political considerations and even commercial rivalries
– conscious or otherwise – which played a hidden role. In
the same way, the tenets of Shi'ism have often been adopted
by peoples who wanted to mark their opposition to the

powers that be. In the sixteenth century, for example, when the Ottoman empire, which was implacably Sunni, was enjoying its greatest expansion and claimed to unite the majority of Muslims under its authority, the Shah of Persia transformed his kingdom into a bastion of Shi'ism. It was a way for him to preserve his empire and for his Persian-speaking subjects to avoid living under the domination of a Turkish-speaking people. But just as the king of England showed his independence by speaking of the Eucharist or Purgatory, so the Shah marked his difference in affirming his attachment to the family of the Prophet, as a guarantee of legitimacy.

Today, genealogical legitimacy retains a certain importance, but another form of legitimacy has been added to it – or sometimes replaced it – which could be called patriotic or combative legitimacy. In the eyes of some Muslims, legitimacy belongs to whoever leads the fight against their enemies. This is similar to the case of General de Gaulle in June 1940: he spoke for France not because he had been elected or because he held effective power, but because he bore the torch in the struggle against the occupier.

This comparison is necessarily approximate. However, it seems to me to hold a useful key to decoding what has been happening in the Arab-Muslim world for several decades – perhaps for far longer, but I prefer to stick to what I myself have noticed as someone born in Lebanon into a family of teachers and journalists, who then emigrated to France and who has never tired of observing the region of his birth and trying to understand and explain it.

From the moment I first opened my eyes, I have seen a procession of different people who believed they possessed patriotic legitimacy, who spoke in the name of their people, or of all Arabs, and sometimes even of all Muslims. The most important of them all was incontestably Gamal Abdel Nasser, who ruled Egypt from 1952 until his death in 1970. I am going to talk at length about him – his meteoric rise and equally spectacular fall and sudden disappearance – because it seems to me that the crisis of legitimacy that Arabs are experiencing today dates from his time. It is a crisis which is contributing to our disordered world and to the drift towards uncontrolled violence and decline.

But before I go into Nasser's career in more detail, I would like to try to work out this notion of patriotic legitimacy more fully using a particular case, a very particular and perhaps even unique case in the modern history of the Muslim world: that of a leader who was able to lead his people out of collapse, thereby meriting his legitimacy as a fighter, and who demonstrated in remarkable ways the strength and uses of such an asset. I am talking of Atatürk.

After the First World War, when the territory of present-day Turkey was divided between various allied armies, and the great powers assembled at Versailles and Sèvres were dealing with peoples and lands without compunction, Atatürk, then an officer in the Ottoman army, dared to say no to the victors. When so many others were bemoaning the unjust decisions which had befallen them, Kemal Pasha took up arms, drove the foreign troops from his country and forced the great powers to revise their plans.

This unusual approach – both the audacity to resist adversaries who were reputed to be invincible and the ability to emerge as victor – meant Atatürk had earned his legitimacy. Having become father of the nation overnight, the former army officer now had a long-term mandate to reshape Turkey and its people as he wished. He undertook this task with gusto. He brought an end to the Ottoman dynasty, abolished the caliphate, proclaimed the separation of religion and state, established strict secularism, demanded that his people Europeanise, replaced the Arabic alphabet with the Roman one, obliged men to shave and women to take off their veils, and exchanged his own traditional headdress for an elegant Western-style hat.

And his people followed him. They let him shake up their behaviour and their beliefs without too much objection. Why? Because he had given them back their pride. Someone who has restored a people's dignity can get them to accept many things. He can impose sacrifices and restrictions on them and can even behave tyrannically. He will still be listened to, defended and obeyed. Not for ever, but for a long time. Even when he takes on religion, his fellow citizens still won't abandon him. In politics, religion is not an end in itself, but one consideration among many. Legitimacy is not accorded to the most devout, but to whoever fights the same fight as the people.

Few people in the East saw any sort of contradiction in the fact that Atatürk fought with great determination against the Europeans while his dream was to Europeanise Turkey. He was not fighting against this or that group; he was fighting in order to be treated with respect, as an equal, as a man, not as a native. As soon as their dignity was restored, Kemal and his people were ready to go a long way down the road to modernity.

The legitimacy which Atatürk attained outlived him and present-day Turkey is still governed in his name. Even those who do not share his convictions still feel the need to display a certain allegiance to him. Nonetheless, one might wonder how long the edifice will hold in the face of growing religious radicalism and with European nervousness. How can the Kemalists convince their people to Europeanise, if the Europeans tell them over and over that they are not European and don't belong among them?

Many Muslim leaders dreamed of following Turkey's example. In Afghanistan, Amanullah, a young king of twenty-six, came to power in 1919 and wanted to follow in Atatürk's footsteps. His army launched an attack on the occupying English forces and succeeded in gaining recognition for his country. Strengthened by the prestige he had won, he embarked on ambitious reforms, forbidding polygamy and the veil, opening modern schools for boys and girls, and encouraging the development of a free press. The experiment lasted ten years, but in 1929 Amanullah was ousted in a conspiracy by traditional chiefs who accused him of impiety. He died in exile in 1960.

Reza Khan's experiment in Persia proved more durable. He was a fervent admirer of Atatürk and, like him, an army officer. He wanted to reproduce the same modernising programme in his country, but he turned out to be unable to

achieve a clean break with the past and instead founded a
new imperial dynasty, the Pahlavis, rather than a European-
style republic, and tried to play on the differences between
the great powers rather than impose a clearly independent
line. He probably lacked Atatürk's talent, though in his
defence the discovery of oil meant there was little chance of
the great powers letting Iran run its own affairs. In order to
remain in power, the dynasty was forced to ally itself first
with the British and then with the Americans; in other
words, with those nations whom the Iranian people viewed
as the enemies of their prosperity and dignity.

This is a counter-example to that of Atatürk. A leader
who appears to be the protégé of opposing powers will be
denied legitimacy and everything he attempts will be discredited. If he wants to modernise the country, the people will
oppose modernisation. If he wants to emancipate women,
the streets will be full of veils in protest.

Many sensible reforms have failed because they bear the
hallmark of a hated power. And conversely, many senseless
acts have been applauded because they bear the seal of
combative legitimacy. This holds good regardless of where
the situation arises. When a proposal is put to the vote, the
electorate votes not so much on its content as on the confidence they do or do not accord to the person who has put it
forward. Regret and second thoughts only come later.

3

In Arab countries, the Turkish experiment received a more qualified welcome than elsewhere in the Muslim world. Atatürk's bold reforms were certainly a source of inspiration for modernising elements of society, such as the Tunisian leader Habib Bourguiba, but there was also in Turkish nationalism a predisposition to distrust the Arabs, which made them unreceptive to his ideas.

For the wish to make Turkey more European was also a wish to make it less Arab. The breakup of the Ottoman empire during the First World War had begun to look like a divorce between the Sultan's Arab and Turkish subjects. When the Hashemites in Mecca raised the standard of revolt in 1916, encouraged by the English, one of their declared objectives was that the dignity of the caliph, a title to which the Ottoman sovereigns had laid claim for four hundred years, should return to the Arabs. Freed from the Turkish yoke, the people of the Prophet would at last be able to reconnect with their past glories.

Turkish nationalists displayed similar resentments: if we have not been able to progress, they said in essence, it is because we have been dragging the Arabic millstone around

for centuries; it's high time we got rid of that complicated
alphabet, those outmoded traditions, this archaic mentality;
and, some added more quietly, that religion. 'The Arabs
want to separate from us? So much the better! Good riddance!
Let them go!'

They didn't stop at changing their alphabet; they undertook to purge the Turkish language of vocabulary of Arabic
origin. These terms were very numerous and widespread,
more so than in Spanish, for example, which borrowed Arab
words mainly for everyday things – the landscape, trees,
food, clothes, instruments, furnitures, trades – whereas its
intellectual and spiritual vocabulary is mainly derived from
Latin. Conversely, the Turkish language mainly borrowed
abstract concepts from Arabic, such as 'faith', 'progress',
'revolution', 'republic', 'literature', 'poetry' and 'love'.

Which is to say that this acrimonious divorce was a separation of both body and soul.

Born at the same time, under the same roof so to speak, but
with little mutual sympathy, Turkish and Arab nationalism
were to have extremely different destinies. The first was born
an adult, the second was never able to become one. It is true
that they did not come into the world with the same advantages or the same restrictions.

The Turks had long governed an immense empire which
had gradually slipped away from them. Some territories had
been taken or reclaimed by other powers – Russia, France,
England, Austria or Italy – and others had had to be ceded to
renascent peoples: Greeks, Romanians, Bulgarians, Serbs,
Albanians, Montenegrins or, more recently, Arabs. Atatürk

told his compatriots that, rather than crying over the provinces they had lost, they should try to save what they could;
make their own national territory where a majority spoke
their language, principally Anatolia and a narrow band of land
in Europe around Istanbul; consolidate their hegemony there,
even if it was at the expense of other nationalities who lived
alongside them; and unceremoniously abandon the trappings
of the Ottoman past in order to begin a new life in new garb.

For the Arabs, the creation of a national homeland was on
the agenda too, but was infinitely more difficult to realise
than for the Turks. Uniting in a single state all the Arabic-
speaking peoples who lived between the Atlantic and the
Persian Gulf was a Herculean undertaking. The Hashemites
were doomed to failure, as were Nasser and all the Arab
nationalists – as would Atatürk himself have been if he had
set himself such an ambitious task.

With hindsight, it may seem as though the enterprise
should never have been attempted, but just after the First
World War it did not seem so absurd. The Ottoman period
had only just come to an end, during which almost all these
countries had effectively been united under the rule of the
same Turkish sultan: why could they not be united again
under an Arabic monarch? In addition, it matched the spirit
of the times. Italian unification had been achieved by Cavour
in 1861 and Germany had been united by Bismarck in 1871.
These events were still relatively recent and the memory of
them was still vivid. Why should Arab unity have been
impossible?

Today, the prospect of forging a single country from Iraq,
Syria, Lebanon, Jordan, Libya, Algeria, Sudan and Saudi

Arabia seems like pure fantasy. But then, none of these countries existed. When their names appeared on maps, they were
geographical regions or administrative units, sometimes
provinces of vanished empires; none of them constituted a
separate state. Arab countries which could claim a contin-
uous history were rare: Morocco, though it was then under
a French protectorate; Egypt, though it was under English
control; and Yemen, whose archaic monarchy kept it apart
from the rest of the world.

Therefore, if it was madness to advocate Arab unity, it
was equal madness not to advocate it. Some historical
dilemmas cannot be resolved, even by the most exceptional
characters. The Arab world was destined to fight with
passion and ferocity to realise its dream of unity, and
destined to fail.

It is in the light of this insoluble dilemma that we can try to
understand Nasser's tragedy and all the dramas that have
stemmed from it down to the present. Thirty-five years
before the advent of the Egyptian leader, the Arabs had been
seduced by another character who, in some circles, has
remained legendary: the Hashemite prince Faisal (the same
Faisal to whom Lawrence of Arabia was adviser and to some
extent mentor). The son of the Sharif of Mecca, he dreamed
of an Arab kingdom with him as sovereign which would
bring together in the first instance the whole of the Middle
East as well as the Arabian peninsula. The British promised it
to him in return for the Arab uprising against the Ottomans,
just as they promised to recognise his father as caliph; and at
the end of the Great War, he went to the Paris Peace

Conference along with Colonel Lawrence to get the backing of the great powers for his plans.

During his time in Paris, he met Chaim Weizmann, an important figure in the Zionist movement who would become the first president of the state of Israel thirty years later. On 3 January 1919, the two men signed an astonishing document boasting of the blood ties and close historical links between their two peoples and stipulating that if the great independent kingdom desired by the Arabs were created, it would encourage the settlement of the Jews in Palestine.

But that kingdom never saw the light of day. The great powers judged that the peoples of the region were not up to the task of governing themselves and decided to grant Great Britain a mandate over Palestine, the West Bank and Iraq, and France a mandate over Syria and Lebanon. A furious Faisal decided to follow Atatürk's path in trying to put a fait accompli before the great powers. Having declared himself king of Syria, he formed a government in Damascus which the majority of Arab political movements joined. But France had no intention of allowing herself to be deprived of the territory which she had been granted. She immediately dispatched an expeditionary force, which easily defeated Faisal's weak forces and seized his capital in July 1920. The only battle took place near the village of Maysaloun, a name that has remained in patriotic memory as a symbol of frustration, impotence, betrayal and mourning.

Having lost his short-lived Syrian kingdom, the Hashemite emir obtained the Iraqi throne under British supervision as a consolation prize, but his prestige was for ever damaged. He died at the age of fifty in 1933 during a stay in

Switzerland. Lawrence died two years later in a motorbike accident.

There would never again be an agreement between Arabs and Jews like that of 1919, a global one which took into account the aspirations of both peoples, endeavouring to reconcile and even unite them. The Jewish colonisation of Palestine would happen against the wishes of the Arabs, who would continue to oppose it with equal amounts of rage and impotence.

When the state of Israel was born in May 1948, its neighbours refused to recognise it and tried to smother it while it was still in the cradle. Their armies entered Palestine only to be beaten one after the other by Jewish troops who were less numerous but better trained, strongly motivated and commanded by competent officers. Israel's four neighbours had to sign armistice agreements: Egypt in February 1949, Lebanon in March, Jordan in April and Syria in July.

This unexpected defeat was a major political shock for the Arab world. Public opinion was outraged, furious at the Israelis, the British and the French, and to some extent the Russians and Americans, who had been quick to recognise Israel; but more than anything, these people were angry with their own leaders, as much for the way in which they had conducted the battle as for their resigned acceptance of defeat. On 14 August 1949, less than a month after signing the armistice, the Syrian president and prime minister were ousted in a coup d'état and summarily executed. In Lebanon, the former prime minister Riad el-Solh, who was away on business during the war and the armistice, was assassinated in

July 1951 by nationalist militants. Five months later, King
Abdullah of Jordan fell in his turn to an assassin's bullet.
Egypt also experienced a wave of attacks and violent demon-
strations, which began with the assassination of Prime
Minister Nokrashi Pasha and ended with the coup d'état of
July 1952. In less than four years, all the Arab leaders who
had accepted the armistice had either lost power or lost their
lives.

In this context, the advent of Nasser was greeted with huge
anticipation and his nationalist rhetoric quickly whipped up
enthusiasm. The Arabs had been dreaming for so long of a
man who would emerge to lead them confidently towards
the realisation of their dreams – unity, true independence,
economic development, social advancement, and above all
restored dignity. They wanted Nasser to be that man; they
believed in him, followed him, loved him. His failure would
shake them profoundly, making them lose all confidence in
their leaders for a long time, and in their own future.

4

Responsibility for Nasser's failure is widely shared. It is true that he was violently opposed by the Western powers, Israel, the oil-producing monarchies, the Muslim Brotherhood, liberals, and also at certain points by Arab communists. But none of his enemies contributed as much to the downfall of Nasserism as Nasser himself.

The man was not a democrat, which is putting it very mildly indeed. He established a single-party system with 99 per cent plebiscites, a ubiquitous secret police, and internment camps where Islamists rubbed shoulders with Marxists, common criminals and unfortunate members of the public who had spoken out ill-advisedly. His nationalism was strongly coloured by xenophobia, which caused the end of a fruitful, centuries-old coexistence between countless Mediterranean communities – Italians, Greeks, Maltese, Jews, Syro-Lebanese Christians – especially in Alexandria. His management of the economy was a model of absurdity and incompetence: one of his regular practices was to appoint as head of a nationalised industry some military man he wanted to reward or move sideways – not the best way to ensure it was effectively run. The army itself, which Nasser

had built up at great cost with help from the Soviets, and
which appeared formidable, collapsed in just a few hours on
5 June 1967 when faced with the Israelis. The Egyptian president had fallen into a trap set by his enemies which he had
been unable to avoid.

I think I have listed most of the charges that can be made
against him, but it is important to add that Nasser was more
than just this. His ascent was probably the most significant
event in Arab history for centuries. So many leaders since
then have committed acts of folly in the hope of occupying
the place in Arab hearts that he once occupied. The megalo-
maniac adventures of Saddam Hussein are incomprehensible
unless one bears in mind that his references to Nebuchad-
nezzar and Saladin were nothing but vain, pompous rhetoric
– his only real ambition was to become a second Nasser.
Many others besides him have dreamt the same thing; some
still dream of it, even though times have changed, and even
though Pan-Arabism, support for the Third World and
socialism have lost their appeal.

In the early 1950s, the Arab world was just beginning to
leave the colonial era behind: the Maghreb was still under
French authority; the Gulf emirates depended on the British
crown; and if some countries had obtained their independence, it was independence in name only for several of them.
That was especially the case in Egypt, where the English
made and unmade governments without paying too much
heed to King Faruk, whose prestige in the eyes of his
people was in perpetual decline. They were irritated by
his lifestyle, the corruption of his entourage, his supposed
eagerness to please the English, and also, after 1948, on

account of his army's humiliating defeat at the hands of
the Israelis.

The 'Free Officers' who took power in Cairo in July 1952
promised to repair all these affronts at once: bringing an end
to the old regime, completing independence by doing away
with British influence and retaking Palestine from the Jews.
These were objectives which corresponded to the aspirations
of the broad mass of Egyptian people and of all Arabs.

Since Egypt was, according to the phrase used at the time,
the Arabs' 'big sister', her experience was very closely
observed.

The Egyptian coup d'état passed off peacefully, and even
with a certain generosity. The deposed king was escorted to
his yacht with military honours and is even said to have been
allowed to take his precious collection of carved walking
sticks with him. He spent the rest of his life between the
Côte d'Azur, Switzerland and Italy, far from any political
activity. For a year the monarchy was not even abolished,
since the crown prince, who was only a few months old,
remained the nominal head of state.

No dignitary of the old regime was killed or given a long
prison sentence. They were stripped of their property, titles
and privileges, but their lives were spared. And while some
of them chose to go into exile, most of them stayed at home
and were barely even concerned. The famous singer Oum
Kalsoum, guilty of having sung in praise of the ousted king,
was taken off air the day after the coup by zealous military
men. She complained to a journalist friend, who immediately told Nasser, and the ban was lifted at once. It was not

long before she was the favourite singer of the new regime.

This good-natured aspect of the Egyptian revolution warrants favourable comparison with so many other events of the same sort which have happened throughout history and which were accompanied by a bloodbath – think of Oliver Cromwell in England, the France of Robespierre, Lenin's Russia, or, closer in time and place, the overthrow of the monarchies in Iraq, Ethiopia and Iran.

But it is worth qualifying this assessment. If Nasser was not a bloody tyrant, neither was he a pacifist. While it is true that the pashas of the old regime all died peacefully in their beds, other political enemies on the right and left whom he judged to be a threat to his power were hanged, shot or killed, and many others died under torture. In addition, Nasser's brand of nationalism always displayed, in his rhetoric as well as in his decisions, a systematic hostility towards everything which was non-native to Egyptian society.

My intention here is not to pass an ethical judgement, even if I have one and it strikes me as legitimate to form one. I am thinking especially of the example that Nasser could have set for those who came after him. He was a model for the Arab world as well as for the whole Muslim world and Africa. As a result, everything he said and did had an educational value for hundreds of millions of people of all conditions across these countries. Few leaders reach such a summit, and only the best of them are conscious of the heavy responsibility that comes with this privilege, especially when it is a case of tracing the path for a new or renascent nation.

An eloquent example from our own time is that of Nelson Mandela. Borne on a powerful wave of support, with an

aura of glamour conferred by his long years of imprison-
ment, he was in a position to call the shots. His people
scrutinised his every word and gesture. If he had voiced
bitterness, settled scores with his jailers, punished everyone
who supported or tolerated apartheid, no one could have
blamed him. If he had wanted to remain president of his
country until his dying breath and governed autocratically,
no one could have stopped him. But he was careful to give
very different signals quite explicitly. He did not just pardon
his persecutors, he made a point of visiting the widow of
former prime minister Verwoerd, one of the architects of
segregation, to tell her that the past was over and that she
too had a place in the new South Africa. The message was
clear: I, Mandela, who suffered persecution under a racist
regime and who did more than anyone else to put an end to
this abomination, made a point, even though I am president, of going to sit under the roof of the man who had me
thrown in prison, to drink tea with his wife. So none of my
supporters should feel they have a right to raise the stakes for
militancy or revenge.

Symbols are potent, and when they come from someone
so eminent, so respected and admired, they can sometimes
alter the course of history.

For a number of years, Nasser found himself in such a position. If he had wanted to, if his political culture and his
temperament had inclined him in that direction, he could
have moved Egypt and the whole of his region towards
greater democracy and greater respect for individual freedom,
and doubtless towards peace and development.

It is easy to forget today that in the early decades of the twentieth century, major Arab and Muslim countries had a lively parliamentary culture, a free press and relatively open elections, enthusiastically supported by the people. That was the case not only in Turkey or Lebanon, but also in Egypt, Syria, Iraq and Iran, so it was not inevitable that they would all succumb to tyrannical or authoritarian regimes.

When he came to power in a country with a very imperfect democratic life, Nasser could have reformed the system, making it accessible to other strata of society, establishing a state in which the rule of law prevailed, putting an end to corruption, nepotism and foreign interference. The population, all classes and shades of opinion together, would probably have followed him down that path. He chose instead to abolish the system entirely and set up a single-party regime, on the pretext that the nation had to be rallied round the objectives of the revolution and that any dissent or division would open a breach for his enemies to exploit.

Of course, history cannot be remade. Having come to power in a bold surprise attack, the young Egyptian colonel – a devoted patriot and an honest man, gifted with intelligence and charisma but without great historical or moral sense – followed his inclination, which matched the spirit of the times. In the early 1950s, conventional wisdom strongly urged him to act in the way he did. Egypt had for several generations been haunted by English machinations, and Nasser was rightly convinced that he had to be extremely firm and vigilant, as otherwise the British would not hesitate to contrive a way to reclaim the prize that had been taken from his people.

The spectacle of the world in the aftermath of the July 1952 coup d'état would only have confirmed Nasser in this view. Everyone was looking at Iran, where prime minister Mossadegh, a Swiss-trained lawyer who was as patriotic as Nasser but a supporter of pluralist democracy, was tussling with the Anglo-Iranian Oil Company. This company paid tiny amounts to the Iranian state, determining them itself as it saw fit. Mossadegh claimed half their revenues for his country. When he received a flat refusal, he got parliament to vote through the nationalisation of the company. The British response was devastatingly effective. They imposed a world embargo on Iranian oil, which no one dared buy. Very soon the country was running out of all resources and its economy was suffocating. In the first year following the Egyptian revolution, the world watched as Mossadegh was brought to his knees and finally fell from power in August 1953. The shah, who had briefly been in voluntary exile, returned in force and stayed for the next twenty-five years.

It was that same summer that Egypt's Free Officers decided to depose the infant king, abandoning any desire to establish a constitutional monarchy and creating an authoritarian republic instead.

In assessing the factors which could have influenced a decision or sparked a conflict, it is never possible to draw a straight line from cause to effect. Many different elements come into play in attempting to understand Nasser's choices, determining the direction the Egyptian revolution took and also in large measure the march of Arab nationalism towards the peaks and then towards the precipice. Besides the far from negligible personal factor, we should also bear in mind various developments which occurred during these years, some directly linked to the Cold War, others to the breakup of Europe's old colonial empires and the emergence of a nationalistic support for the Third World, which was generally anti-Western and attracted to the Soviet model of a single party and a planned economy.

In theory, Nasser could have decided to take a different course. In reality, given the temper of the times and the balance of power, that would have been difficult – and risky.

5

In 1956, during the Suez Crisis, Nasser became the idol of the wider Arab world, because he dared to throw down the gauntlet to the colonial European powers and emerged victorious from the confrontation.

In July of that year, during a rally in Alexandria to celebrate the fourth anniversary of the revolution, he unexpectedly declared, in a speech broadcast live, the nationalisation of the Franco-British Suez Canal Company, a symbol of the foreign stranglehold on his country. This speech left his audience delirious, and the rest of the world reeling. London and Paris were irate and spoke of piracy and acts of war, and warned of the risks of disturbing international trade.

Overnight, the 38-year-old Egyptian colonel was propelled to the centre of the international stage. The entire world seemed to divide into his supporters and critics. In one camp were the peoples of the Third World, the Non-Aligned Movement, the Soviet bloc, as well as the growing sector of Western opinion that wished to draw a line under the colonial era, either for reasons of principle or of cost. In the other camp were Great Britain, France and Israel; so too, though more discreetly, were certain conservative Arab leaders who feared the destabilising influence of Nasser in their own countries; among them was the Iraqi prime minister, Nuri es-Said, who advised his British counterpart, Anthony Eden, to 'Hit him! – Hit him now, and hit him hard!' Fresh in everyone's memory was the fate inflicted on Mossadegh. It seemed inconceivable that the Egyptian leader would not be penalised in the same way, so that the West would retain control of this important seaway and at the same time set an example.

A decision was indeed taken to hit him hard. At the end of October, a two-part operation was set in motion: the Israelis initiated a land offensive in Sinai, and British and French commandos parachuted into the zone around the canal. Militarily, Nasser was beaten, but politically he was about to score a triumph, thanks in particular to a historic coincidence which neither he nor his enemies had foreseen.

On the very day on which Paris and London delivered an ultimatum to Cairo in advance of their attack, a new Hungarian government led by Imre Nagy declared its return to pluralist democracy, thereby openly rebelling against Moscow's hegemony. That occurred on Tuesday, 30 October 1956. In the days that followed, the two dramas unfolded in parallel: while the Royal Air Force was bombing Cairo Airport, and French and British parachutists were dropping from the skies above Port Said, Soviet tanks were bloodily trying to crush student demonstrators in Budapest.

Nowhere was there more fury over this coincidence than in Washington. The fiercely anti-Communist administration of President Eisenhower and the two Dulles brothers – John

Foster, the secretary of state, and Alan, the director of the CIA – saw in the events in Hungary a major milestone in the confrontation between the two world blocs. The Soviet leadership was clearly in a state of disarray. The process of de-Stalinisation which they had initiated had turned against them. To maintain their domination of Central and Eastern Europe, the only choice they had left was brute force. The time was ripe for the US to isolate the Russians, undermine their credibility on the international stage, and inflict a major political defeat.

By launching a military campaign against Egypt at this precise moment, the British, French and Israelis were giving the Soviets an unimagined opportunity to deflect the world's attention away from their own punitive operation. The Americans were incensed. Whereas in the summer they had given their friends to believe that they would let them get on with it, they now begged them to stop, to cancel the operation and withdraw their troops. Suez could wait!

But the operation was already under way, and Eden neither could nor would call it off. Insistent calls from Washington made no impression. He believed he knew his habitually reluctant allies very well. Initially, they would drag their heels and find pretexts not to intervene – the English always had to go first, encouraging and prodding them – but the Americans would eventually get involved and fight better than anyone, he thought. But what efforts Churchill had had to expend in order to drag them into the war against Hitler! Hadn't Great Britain had to hold on virtually alone for two and a half years before the United States joined the fray? In the Iranian crisis, the same scenario had repeated itself. Left to themselves, the Americans would have put up with Mossadegh's government and their nationalisation of oil. They had, moreover, insisted that Great Britain accept a compromise which took into account the national aspirations of the Iranians. Once again it had been necessary for Churchill, Eden and many other representatives to go to discuss this at the White House and the State Department, explaining and arguing before the Americans would agree to act. Once again, US intervention had proved decisive; indeed, it was they who had so effectively orchestrated the overthrow of Mossadegh. Eden predicted that in the Suez Crisis the same thing would happen. In the end, Washington would understand that the fight against Communism is the same, whether in Egypt, Hungary, Iran, Korea or elsewhere.

The prime minister was sorely mistaken. Not only did the Americans have no intention of following him in his adventure, they were so irritated that they intended to publicly humiliate him. Since Eden refused to understand that his stupid little war was playing into the hands of the Soviets, he would be treated like an enemy – unheard of in two centuries of Anglo-American relations. The American Treasury began to sell huge quantities of sterling, which led the currency to fall, and when some of the Arab countries decided no longer to supply oil to France and Great Britain out of solidarity with Egypt, the Americans refused to make up the shortfall. At the UN Security Council, the US delegation sponsored a resolution demanding the cessation of military operations. When Paris and London exercised their veto, the same proposal was submitted to the General

Assembly, which voted massively in favour. Even the large Anglo-Saxon countries of the Commonwealth, such as Canada and Australia, made clear to Eden that he could no longer count on their support.

In the end, the British leader and his French counterpart, Guy Mollet, gave in and recalled their troops. Despite their military success on the ground, their political defeat was complete. Having behaved as though they still possessed vast world empires, the two European powers had suffered a devastating blow. The Suez Crisis sounded the death knell for the colonial era; thereafter, the world entered a new age, with different powers and different rules.

As a result of revealing this seismic change and emerging victorious, Nasser became a major figure on the world stage overnight – and for the Arabs, one of the greatest heroes in their history.

6

The Nasser era did not last long: eighteen years at a generous estimate, from his coup d'état in July 1952 to his death in September 1970; and just eleven years if you count only the period during which the majority of Arab people believed in him, from the nationalisation of the Suez Canal in July 1956 until the Six Day War in June 1967.

Was it a golden age? Certainly not if you judge him on his record. Nasser was unable to raise his country out of under-development, nor was he able to establish modern political institutions, and his plans for union with other states ended only in failure. The whole thing was crowned with a monu-mental military disaster in the confrontation with Israel in 1967. However, the abiding impression of those years among Arabs is that they were for a time actors in their own history, rather than powerless, insignificant and despised bit-part players, and that they had a leader in whom they saw them-selves reflected. And even if their adored president was not a democrat, had come to power in a military coup and had remained there by means of dubious elections, he appeared legitimate far beyond the borders of his own country, whereas leaders who opposed him appeared illegitimate, never mind that they were the heirs of more ancient dynasties or even the descendants of the Prophet.

Under Nasser, Arabs felt as though they had recovered their dignity, and were able to hold their heads high alongside other nations. Until that time, and for generations and indeed centuries, all they had known were defeats, foreign occupations, unfair treaties, capitulation, humiliation and the shame of having sunk so low after having conquered half the world.

Every Arab carries within him the soul of a fallen hero, and the desire for revenge on all those who have treated him with contempt. If he is promised revenge, he listens with a combination of expectation and incredulity. If he is offered revenge, even in part, even in a symbolic form, he is transported.

Nasser had asked his brothers to raise their heads. In their name, he had defied the colonial powers; in their name, he had confronted the 'tripartite aggression'; in their name, he had triumphed. Joy was immediate. Tens of millions of Arabs thereafter could see only him, thought only of him, and swore only by him. They were ready to support him against the entire world, and sometimes even ready to die for him. And, of course, to applaud him endlessly and chant his name with their eyes closed. When he was successful, they blessed him; when he suffered setbacks, they cursed his enemies.

In reality, there were both highs and lows. In hindsight, the Nasser years appear like a rapid game of chess in which the players would occupy a square, move from it when they came under pressure, only to reoccupy it a little later, then perhaps lose a major piece, then quickly take one of their enemy's – until the final confrontation ended in a surprising checkmate.

So, in just this fashion, in February 1958, only fifteen months after the Battle of Suez, Nasser entered Damascus in triumph. Such was his popularity in Syria that its leaders had decided to hand power over to him. A United Arab Republic was declared, made up of a southern province, Egypt, and a northern one, Syria. The old dream of Arab unity seemed to be on the way to becoming a reality. Better still, Nasser's great republic corresponded exactly to the kingdom built eight centuries earlier by Saladin, who, in 1169, had come to power in Cairo, and in 1174 had conquered Damascus, taking the free kingdom of Jerusalem in a pincer movement. (Incidentally, Al-Nasser, 'he who gives victory', was Saladin's surname.)

In the months that followed the declaration of the United Arab Republic, a rebellion broke out in Beirut against President Chamoun, who was accused of supporting the French and British during the Suez Crisis. There were calls for his resignation, and some Nasser supporters even advocated that Lebanon should become part of the Egypto-Syrian state. Several other countries began to experience an intense ferment of nationalist activity.

In order to confront these challenges, the pro-Western kingdoms of Iraq and Jordan – which were both governed by young sovereigns of the Hashemite dynasty aged just twenty-three – decided to declare in their turn a united Arab kingdom. But this 'counter-union' lasted only a few weeks. On 14 July 1958, a bloody coup overthrew the Iraqi monarchy and put an end to the project. The whole royal family was massacred and Nasser's old enemy, Nuri es-Said, was lynched by the mob in the streets of Baghdad.

Nasser's nationalist tide seemed to be well on the way to overwhelming the entire Arab world from the ocean to the Gulf, and at high speed. Never had the theory of the domino effect worked so quickly. Every monarchy was shaken and on the point of falling, especially that of King Hussein, who seemed to be facing an identical fate to that of his unfortunate Iraqi cousin.

Washington and London consulted each other on the morning of 14 July and agreed on an immediate response. The very next day, American marines landed on Lebanese beaches; two days later, British commandos arrived in Jordan. It was a way of telling Nasser that if he went one step further, he would enter into direct military conflict with the West.

This response had the desired effect. The nationalist wave ebbed. In Lebanon, the rebellion lost momentum and President Chamoun was able to serve the rest of his term. In Jordan, King Hussein was not ousted; various threats still lay ahead for him – military rebellions, attacks on his person and on those close to him – but by surviving this first attack, he was able to save his throne.

Nasser was to suffer two further serious reversals. In Iraq, an internal struggle soon began among the architects of the coup, between those who wanted to align themselves with Cairo and those who wanted to keep their distance. Nasser's friends were beaten and ousted. Rather than joining the United Arab Republic, the strong man of the new regime,

General Abdel-Karim Kassem, presented himself as the
champion of a specifically Iraqi revolution and clearly
anchored on the left. He thereby became Nasser's sworn
enemy overnight and a struggle to the death between the
two men began. On 7 October 1959, in central Baghdad,
Kassem's armoured car was riddled with bullets. Kassem got
away with only scratches; his attacker, who was wounded in
the leg, managed to escape across the border to seek refuge
in Syria. He was a 22-year-old militant nationalist by the
name of Saddam Hussein.

Nasser's other failure would turn out to be yet more
devastating. At dawn on 28 September 1961, a military coup
took place in Damascus. The restoration of Syrian independence and the end of the union with Cairo were declared.
Arab nationalists denounced this 'separatist' act and accused
those involved in the putsch of being puppets of colonialism,
Zionism, reactionary forces and the oil-producing monarchies. But no one was unaware at the time that the Syrian
population was finding it more and more difficult to tolerate
Egyptian control, not least because it was exercised through
the secret services. Like Baghdad, Damascus is one of the
historical capitals of the Muslim world; Baghdad was the seat
of the Abassid caliphate, while Damascus was the seat of the
Umayyad caliphate. Both were willing to be a sister to Cairo,
but not her servant. Such feelings were widespread
throughout the population, especially among the urban
bourgeoisie and landowners, whom Nasser's nationalisations
had ruined.

The Egyptian leader's star seemed irredeemably tarnished.
His popularity might have remained intact among the masses

in most Arab countries, but his enemies, both in the region and in the West, breathed more easily, believing that the initial nationalist wave was now no more than a memory.

But all of a sudden, the wave broke again, this time stronger and wider than before. During the summer of 1962, an independent Algeria elected as its leader Ahmed Ben Bella, a fervent admirer of Nasser. In September, Free Officers, inspired by the example of Egypt, overthrew the most reactionary monarchy of all, that of the imams in Yemen. A Yemeni republic was declared, to which Nasser promised every assistance. Soon thousands of Egyptian soldiers were arriving in the south of the Arabic peninsula, causing the oil-producing kingdoms to tremble.

On 8 February 1963, Arab nationalist officers seized power in Baghdad. Kassem was summarily executed and his body displayed on television. The new head of state was Colonel Abdessalam Aref, one of Nasser's faithful allies. A month later, on 8 March, a similar coup d'état took place in Damascus, in which the end of separatism was declared, along with the aim of recreating a union with Egypt and Iraq, perhaps also Yemen and Algeria, and even, in the future, Lebanon, Libya, Kuwait, Sudan, Saudi Arabia, and so on.

Suddenly, within a few months, Nasser's dream of Arabic unity seemed revived, and more vigorous than ever. Iraq and Syria's new leaders went to Cairo to negotiate the terms of a new union, a project which was solemnly announced on 17 April 1963. Thus, a powerful Arab state was about to be born, uniting the three great imperial capitals, Cairo, Baghdad and Damascus. Arab nationalism seemed to be on the verge of an unprecedented historical triumph. Its supporters were delirious, and its enemies alarmed. Neither group could have imagined then how close the denouement was.

7

The new ebb in support for Nasser turned out to be as rapid as the original surge had been. In the weeks following the agreement about the new union, it became known that the Cairo negotiations had in fact gone very badly. The Syrian and Iraqi leaders, who all belonged to the pan-Arabic Ba'ath ('resurrection') party, wanted a partnership in which Nasser was the head of the new state, but which gave them the real power on the ground. Remembering the mistakes made during the first attempt at a union, they did not want their countries to be governed by some viceroy subservient to the Egyptian leader. Nasser, for his part, had no desire to be the nominal president of a state dominated by these Ba'athists for whom he had neither trust nor sympathy. They may have been the architects of the two coups, but it was Nasser who was the standard bearer of Arab unity; it was in him that the people saw their aspirations reflected, and him alone whom they desired as their leader. It was not long before this disagreement degenerated into a violent trial of strength. In Baghdad, the confrontation went provisionally in favour of the Egyptian president, but when Nasser's supporters in Syria rose up against the Ba'athists, the rebellion was violently suppressed and the death toll ran into hundreds.

In Yemen, the royalists, aided by Saudi Arabia, furiously opposed the new republican regime and succeeded in hampering the efforts of the Egyptian expeditionary force. Their mission turned to disaster militarily, financially and also morally when some of the soldiers involved started behaving not as liberators but as occupiers, and even looters.

Another blow for Nasser came in June 1965, when his friend Ben Bella was overthrown in a military coup; Algeria's new president, Houari Boumediene, was quick to distance himself from Cairo.

The backlash was on a massive scale. Even beyond the Arab world, the Egyptian president lost some of his closest allies. The Ghanaian Kwame Nkrumah, an advocate of African unity and a fervent admirer of Nasser – so much so that he had given his son the first name Gamal – was overthrown in February 1966 by a military coup. Then it was the turn of the Indonesian Sukarno, a standard-bearer in the Non-Aligned Movement; on 11 March 1966, he was forced to cede power to the pro-American General Suharto.

Finally, as if to complete Nasser's isolation, his last faithful ally among the Arab leaders, the Iraqi president Abdessalam Aref, died on 13 April 1966 in circumstances which have never been fully explained. He was visiting the south of the country near Bassora when his helicopter malfunctioned and went out of control. Suddenly the door opened and the president fell out; his head hit the ground and he was killed instantly.

★   ★   ★

This bizarre accident could not have come at a worse moment for Nasser, who more than ever needed trustworthy allies, since the political landscape of the region was beginning to be populated with movements and individuals which were challenging his authority, such as the Ba'ath party or Fatah, a newcomer on the scene.

When on 1 January 1965 a communiqué announced the first military operation by a previously unknown Palestinian organisation, the Egyptian president knew at once that this action was not solely aimed against Israel or Jordan, but also against him. Up until that point, the Palestinians had been Nasser's most enthusiastic supporters, because it was they who had had to leave their homes when the state of Israel was created, and who hoped to return there through an Arab victory. In the meantime, most of them were living in refugee camps and had placed all their hopes in Nasser.

Nasser himself never missed an opportunity to lambast the 'Zionist enemy', to bring up the setback suffered by Israel during the Suez Crisis or to promise fresh victories to come. The Palestinians had been persuaded that the Egyptian president's nationalist mobilisation was the only route which would permit them to win. But some of them were beginning to grow impatient. They had had enough of their struggle constantly being sacrificed to other priorities and constantly deferred. Nasser was clearly in no hurry to go to war against Israel. First he had to achieve Arab unity, drive out colonialism, consolidate the socialist economy, overcome reactionary regimes and so on. The founders of Fatah believed that the Palestinians ought to conduct their own fight according to their own agenda. Their first communiqué

amounted to a declaration of independence – and also one of
defiance – with regard to other Arab leaders and in particular
with regard to the most prominent of them, Nasser.

Mockery of Nasser was also growing in various quarters.
Hadn't he had enough time since 1956 to prepare a war
against Israel? Hadn't he been sufficiently well armed by the
Soviets? Hadn't he acquired planes, tanks and even subma-
rines? Wasn't it strange that not a single shot had been fired
against the common enemy in ten years?

The Egyptian president was not insensitive to these criticisms. After all, his accession to power had come about as a
direct reaction to the Arabs' defeat in 1948 and he had arrived
promising to repair that affront. This was the context in
which he had become a hero. In 1956, he had given the
crowds a foretaste of the promised victory, and in his speeches
he constantly held up the glittering prospect of other battles
to come. The crowds listened to him and trusted him; they
did not expect him to launch a battle before he was ready,
but his credit had its limits. Especially if others were now
taking up arms against Israel.

And that is precisely what happened after 1 January 1965.
One Fatah operation succeeded another and its press releases
were reported in the media.

The most militant sector of Arab public opinion cheered;
and in the conservative monarchies too the exploits of the
Fedayeen were admired, and compared favourably to the
duplicitous rhetoric of Nasser, 'who prefers to send his
troops to fight in Yemen rather than in Negev, Jaffa or
Galilee'.

★   ★   ★

The Egyptian president's position became yet more awkward when Israel began to react violently to Fatah's attacks. On the night of 11–12 November 1966, an Israeli border patrol encountered a landmine which went off, killing three soldiers and injuring six others. Believing that the Palestinian commandos who planted it came from the village of es-Samu in the West Bank – which then belonged to the kingdom of Jordan – the Israelis launched a massive reprisal attack on 13 November. But instead of encountering the Fedayeen, they came face to face with a detachment of the Hashemite army. A violent battle ensued, which at one point involved the air force. Sixteen Jordanian soldiers were killed as well as the Israeli colonel directing the operation. In the village, dozens of houses were destroyed and three civilians killed.

The Israeli reaction was universally condemned or at least strongly criticised, not just by the Arabs, Soviets and non-aligned countries, which were in the habit of condemning everything that Israel did, but also by the Americans, who could not understand why anyone would want to destabilise one of the rare moderate regimes in the Arab world, which had always been the least hostile to the Jewish state.

In Israel itself, many people felt that the operation had been misguided and also badly executed. Moshe Dayan, the former chief of the armed forces and future defence minister, asked why it was Jordan that had been attacked when everyone knew it was Syria that was financing and arming the Fedayeen. The idea that the wrong target had been hit was quickly admitted by most leaders, who promised that next time they would come knocking on the 'right door'.

In fact, attention was turning more and more towards Damascus, as a result of its support for Palestinian militants and also because of the increasingly frequent engagements between Syrian artillery on the Golan Heights and Israeli troops stationed in the Galilee settlements. On 7 April 1967, a minor border skirmish escalated into an aerial combat in the skies above Damascus. Six Syrian planes were shot down.

All these events reverberated more and more in Arabic public opinion, where the same questions kept arising: what was Nasser doing? What was the Egyptian army doing? When people didn't ask these questions spontaneously, some sectors of the media took it upon themselves to whisper them in their ears, with a reminder that Nasser ran no risk of being attacked himself, unlike the Jordanians and Syrians, 'since he was hiding like a timid little girl in the skirts of the United Nations' – an allusion to the fact that international observers had been posted in Gaza and all along the Egyptian–Israeli border since the Suez Crisis. This had been a condition of the Israeli forces evacuating Sinai, and Nasser had agreed after obtaining a guarantee from the UN secretary general, the Swede Dag Hammarskjöld, that they would be withdrawn as soon as Cairo requested it.

The accusation of timidity had become a recurring refrain at this time for all Nasser's enemies, on both the right and the left. The Arab media linked to the Jordanian, Saudi and Iranian monarchies – now grouped in an 'Islamic pact' in opposition to the Egyptian president – never missed a chance to draw attention to the disparity between his bellicose words and his actual behaviour. But the official press in Damascus was no less virulent; it no longer held back from describing

Nasser in language previously reserved for pro-Western leaders. It spoke of cowardice and capitulation, and accused him of leaving the Egyptian army far from the battlefield while the Syrian army was currently at the front, ready to have it out with the enemy and to crush them.

Nasser could not stand for this. If it had just been a matter of invective and tirades, then perhaps he could have brushed it off. But tension was mounting in the region, and there was a persistent sound of marching boots. Was military confrontation really on the horizon? He knew that his enemies wanted to catch him out, and he was just as mistrustful of the intentions of Damascus or of the armed Palestinian movements as he was of Tel Aviv and Washington, London, Amman and Riyadh. In private, he told those close to him that a trap was clearly being set and that he would not allow himself to be caught.

Nonetheless, if tension continued to mount and did indeed lead to war, how on earth could he stand idly by? How could the standard-bearer of the Arab nation leave his army on the sidelines if other Arab armies were engaged in fighting with the common enemy?

On 12 May, press agencies reported statements by a high-ranking Israeli military official claiming that his country had decided to overthrow the Syrian regime if it continued to support the Fedayeen. The following day, an Egyptian figure who had hitherto played only a minor role, Anwar Sadat, then president of the parliament, made a brief stop-off in Moscow on the way back from a routine courtesy visit to Mongolia and North Korea. He was expecting to be politely greeted by some civil servant, but in fact some of the USSR's top leaders met him to tell him that, according to their sources, the Israelis had amassed fifteen divisions on their northern border and an invasion of Syria was imminent – 'ten days away at most'. As soon as he returned to Cairo, Sadat went to see Nasser, who had just been given the same information by the Soviet ambassador.

Nasser decided that he had no option but to send his army to Sinai, at the same time requesting that the UN withdraw its contingent, which it did without objection. The Egyptian forces took up position in Gaza and especially Sharm el-Sheikh, which controls the Straits of Tiran and access to the Gulf of Aqaba, through which the Israelis had been receiving deliveries of Iranian oil for years under a secret agreement with the Shah. While this route remained in the hands of international forces, Nasser left it alone, but as soon as his own troops were in place, he could no longer turn a blind eye. He had either to tolerate this traffic or put a stop to it.

The Arab masses who, two weeks earlier, had never heard of the Straits of Tiran, were now demanding that they be closed. The media – both Nasser's supporters and his enemies – were also speaking with one voice. Everyone was aware that closing the straits would inevitably lead to war between Egypt and Israel; but it was a war which everyone wanted, whether to put an end to the state of Israel or to get rid of Nasser.

8

When he received the message about an imminent invasion of Syria, Nasser sent a man he could trust to Damascus: Mahmoud Fawzi, his chief of staff. Fawzi had instructions to show solidarity and offer help, but also to check the veracity of the Soviet intelligence.

On his return, Fawzi summed up the situation in a common Egyptian expression: 'Ma fich haga!' ('Nothing's happening!') 'How can that be?' Nasser asked. The general replied, 'The Israelis are not massed along the border, and the Syrians don't look as though they are expecting an imminent invasion.' Nasser was more puzzled than ever, but there was no longer any turning back. His troops were already deployed in Sinai, the blue helmets were packing up and the temperature of public opinion was rising all the time.

Like many great orators, Nasser was always sensitive to the mood of his audience and, especially when it came to the Arab–Israeli issue, often prisoner of his own rhetoric. In those torrid days of 1967, it was clear that public opinion could no longer be controlled and that the mood of the crowd was dictating the actions of the man whose name they chanted.

When on 22 May he declared that the Straits of Tiran were closed to shipping, the reverberations were greater than at any other moment in his career. That very day, lines of demonstrators formed in Arab cities from the Maghreb to Iraq. One slogan was repeated over and over: 'Yesterday we nationalised the canal, and today we have closed the straits.' With hindsight, this 'we' may provoke a smile, but it translated a genuine feeling. The Arab masses recognised themselves instinctively in Nasser and felt ownership of his political decisions as though they had issued them themselves. On reflection, this was at once both perfectly illusory and profoundly true.

The Egyptian president seemed during those days to be at the peak of his power. The support of the Arab peoples for the coming fight and for the leader who would lead it was so overwhelming that no other leader was able to stand in his way. The most astonishing reaction was that of King Hussein, who had been Nasser's most determined enemy since the Egyptian came to power. Until that point, there had been a struggle without mercy between the two men. Then suddenly, at dawn on Tuesday 30 May, the Hashemite monarch's private plane took off for Cairo, where he told his old enemy that he would put the full resources of his kingdom at his disposal in the coming war. Surprised and still distrustful, Nasser insisted that an officer of the Egyptian high command should be placed at the head of the Jordanian army. King Hussein accepted without protest.

This spectacular turnaround is worth pondering for a moment. The 'little king' was definitely not a demagogue, and he was passionately devoted to the independence of his country. Nor was he a sworn enemy of the Jewish state bent on military revenge. Throughout his long reign, which lasted almost half a century, he refused to yield to Arab taboos concerning relations with the 'Zionist enemy' and he frequently met with Israeli leaders during his travels overseas. He even went so far as to deliver the funeral oration for Yitzhak Rabin in Jerusalem in 1995, calling the man who had conquered the Holy City at his expense 'my friend'.

If in May 1967 he decided to join Nasser, it was because it would have been suicidal to set himself against the patriotic legitimacy of the moment. Not taking part in the coming war would have been disastrous for the Hashemite monarchy, whatever the outcome of the fighting. An Arab victory would have placed Nasser in a position to destroy the Jordanian throne. An Arab defeat would have led to the finger of blame being pointed first at any nation which had refused to fight. From the moment war had become inevitable, King Hussein understood that he would have to fight alongside Egypt, and even under its command. That is how the instinct for legitimacy works. Jordan stood to lose the West Bank, but it was already as good as lost, either to the Israelis or to Arab insurgents, as soon as war broke out. King Hussein could not have continued to govern millions of Palestinians if he had refused to take part in the fight for Palestine.

The king would behave in the same way a quarter of a century later, during the first Gulf War. While the whole of the world joined forces against Saddam Hussein, the Hashemite king rallied to Iraq's support. Was this because he wanted to see him win? Certainly not. Because he believed an Iraqi victory was possible? Absolutely not. It was simply because, at this other crucial turning point in Middle Eastern history, the king preferred to be wrong along with his people, rather than right in opposition to them.

King Hussein's attitude in 1967 is easier to understand if you compare it with that of another of Israel's neighbours, Lebanon. Its leaders took a decision not to participate in the war, which at the time seemed eminently reasonable. But in so doing, they lost their patriotic legitimacy in the eyes of a good proportion of the Lebanese people. As a result, the country became bogged down in a historical quagmire from which it still has not escaped forty years later.

From 1968, armed Palestinian groups began to launch attacks from Lebanon. When the Israelis responded violently and the authorities in Beirut, who were incapable of repelling the attacks of their powerful neighbour, decided to clamp down on the Fedayeen, a section of public opinion sided with the militants rather than their own government. The argument which was repeated endlessly was that the Lebanese army, which hadn't fought against the enemy, should at least not be fighting with those who were.

Lebanon's wisest politicians repeated that the 1967 war was one of the most unthinking acts that the Arab countries had committed in their history; that if Lebanon had taken part alongside Israel's three other neighbours, it would have lost part of its territory, as Egypt, Syria and Jordan did; and that its army would probably have been destroyed without changing the power relations or the outcome of the fighting one iota. No one could seriously take issue with any of this. Nonetheless, a significant proportion of the population no longer recognised itself in its government or its army, and could not tolerate seeing it clamp down on those who were actively engaged in fighting. Some Lebanese, especially those who belonged to Muslim communities and left-wing parties, came to consider the Palestinian fighters as their army, and the regular army as belonging to the Christian parties and the right. That regular army began to fall apart and the state lost control of the country.

The region which suffered most was the south. That was where the Fedayeen had gained a foothold; it was from there that they launched their attacks, and that was where the Israelis hit back. The local population, who were mainly Shi'ite, felt as though they were despised and abandoned, victims caught between the Devil and the deep blue sea. They came in time to curse the Palestinians just as much as the Israelis.

It was from all these resentments that Hezbollah was born. In 1982, the Israeli army, following a war which had seen it get as far as Beirut, decided no longer to confine itself to limited punitive expeditions, but to occupy the south of Lebanon outright in such a way as to firmly close the border. Shi'ite militants, inspired, armed and financed by their fellow Shi'ites in Iran, threw themselves into a resistance movement which turned out to be highly effective from the start. Little by little, the Lebanese, who had long been mocked by other Arabs for having been the only ones not to take part in the fighting, appeared as the only ones who knew how to fight, to the point that they forced the Israeli army to evacuate their country in May 2000, and then held it in check during the war of the summer of 2006.

So, in the years that followed the war of 1967, Israel's three neighbours that took part in the fighting managed to reach arrangements which made their borders with the Jewish state perfectly peaceful: with Egypt and Jordan there were treaties, and with Syria, a *modus vivendi*. Only the fourth neighbour, the one that had not wanted to go to war, was unable to achieve peace. Since then it has been in turmoil. In theory, its leaders in 1967 showed themselves to be reasonable in remaining outside the conflict. In practice, however, the price paid by Lebanon for not taking part in the war was a thousand times more costly than if it had done.

9

I shall close this long parenthesis on the way in which legitimacy functions and return to those days in May and June 1967 when Nasser had taken up, or reacquired, the reins of the Arab nation, promising to lead it towards the hoped-for victory. His armed forces and those of Israel were now face to face.

Having originally planned to attack first, Nasser abandoned the idea, convinced that it would be politically disastrous as the Americans would get involved in force on the Israeli side and the Soviets would be embarrassed. If, by contrast, he allowed himself to *be* attacked, he would immediately find himself in an excellent diplomatic position: the whole world would be with him, not least General de Gaulle's France; and the United States would find it difficult to get fully involved on the side of the aggressor. In any case, he thought the fighting would go on for weeks, encompassing many fronts, and that reinforcements would pour in from all over the Arab world, while the Israelis would inevitably become exhausted. It would all end in a settlement, he imagined, which would constitute a major political victory for Egypt and for him personally.

Of course, Nasser knew this policy would come at a price. By letting the Israelis strike first, he was taking a risk. But, he believed, it was a calculated one. His right-hand man, Marshal Abdel-Hakim Amer, had assured him that even if all of Israel's bombers attacked at once, Egypt would only lose between 10 and 15 per cent of its planes. Within a few days, the Soviets would have replaced them.

What Nasser had completely failed to foresee was that the first blow dealt by the Israelis could wipe out the Egyptian air force. Yet that is what happened on the morning of Monday, 5 June 1967.

Flying at very low altitude, the Israeli bombers attacked all of Egypt's military airports simultaneously, putting runways out of action and destroying planes on the ground. The land army remained intact and could have fought for a long time in Sinai, giving the president the possibility of recovering, replacing his lost aircraft and even preparing a counter-offensive. But Marshal Amer, in a state of panic and confusion, ordered a general retreat, which turned into a rout.

Having put Egypt out of action, the Israeli army turned towards Jerusalem and the West Bank, where it took control following a short street battle; then it turned towards Syria, which retreated from the Golan Heights without much resistance. Within a week, the fighting was over. The victors would call the conflict the Six Day War; for the defeated, it would be above all 'al-anksa' ('the setback'), then quite simply 'the June War'.

These bland names scarcely conceal the extent of the trauma suffered by the Arabs during these days. It is no exaggeration to say that for them, this short war remains the tragic reference point which colours their perception of the world and influences their behaviour.

Following the defeat, one question obsessed all Arabs and many Muslims throughout the world. Everyone framed it in his own way and came up with his own answers, but the substance was the same: how had such a defeat come about?

At first, in order to excuse his failure, Nasser had said that the attack had not come from Israel alone, but in conjunction with the Americans and the British. If this was not true, it was useful in the short term in order to mitigate the despair felt by the Egyptians and the wider Arab world. Being beaten by a great power was infuriating but it was in the order of things, and much less shameful than being beaten by a small state created twenty years earlier, which had a population a tenth the size of Egypt's and a smaller army.

The war of 1967 should have washed away the stain of 1948, when the new Jewish state had stood up to a coalition of its neighbours. It was supposed to demonstrate that the Arabs had regained confidence, had reconnected with their former glory, and that their national renaissance under the aegis of Nasser had at last given them back their rightful place among the nations of the world. Instead of which, this light-ning defeat had taken away their self-esteem and for years to come established a relationship of profound distrust with the rest of the world, which they perceived as a hostile place run by their enemies in which they themselves no longer belonged. They felt that everything which made up their identity was despised and scorned by the rest of the world and – more seriously still – something within them told them that such hatred and scorn were not completely unjustified. This double hatred – of the world and of themselves – explains in large part the destructive and suicidal behaviour which has characterised the past decade.

This behaviour has become such a frequent, even daily, occurrence in Iraq and elsewhere that it has ceased to be shocking. So it seems to me useful to remind ourselves that never before in the history of humanity have we seen such a widespread phenomenon, never have we lived through a period in which hundreds or thousands of men have shown such a propensity to sacrifice their lives. All of the historical parallels which are sometimes cited to relativise this phenomenon are grossly inappropriate. The Japanese kamikaze were, for example, members of a regular army and their attacks were only common during the last year of the war in the Pacific, and they came to a definitive end with the capitulation of their government. And, in Muslim history, members of the Order of the Assassins only attacked clearly defined targets and never killed at random. They allowed themselves to be taken prisoner and executed for their acts, but never took their own lives. Nor did they commit more than a handful of attacks in the course of two centuries, making them resemble Russian revolutionaries of the tsarist period much more closely than today's 'martyrs'.

The despair which fires these martyrs does not date from 1967 or 1948, or the end of the First World War. It is the culmination of a long historical process which no single date or event can adequately encapsulate. It is in the history of a people who have known a great moment of glory followed by a long decline. For two hundred years they have aspired to rise again, but each time they fall back down. Defeats, disappointments and humiliations had followed one after the other until the moment when Nasser appeared. With him, they believed it would once again be possible to get back on their feet, regain their self-esteem and the admiration of others. When they collapsed again in such a spectacular and degrading fashion, the Arabs, and the rest of the Muslim world, had the feeling that they had lost everything irremediably.

Since then, agonising self-examination has been going on, but in an atmosphere of bitterness and fear, and with an excess of faith which poorly masks infinite despair.

Nasser's defeat, followed by his death in September 1970 at the age of fifty-two, encouraged the emergence of various competing political projects that claimed his legacy.

In Egypt itself, power was assumed by Anwar Sadat, a character previously thought dull and timorous, but who in fact turned out to be bold and flamboyant. That was not the strangest aspect of his career, however; pretenders who make themselves inconspicuous while the master is still alive only to reveal themselves as soon as they assume power are legion throughout world history. Strong men love to be surrounded by people who do not oppose them, who do not cast a shadow and who wait for their moment without showing signs of impatience. Nor was the strangest thing about Sadat that he managed in October 1973 to dislodge the Israeli army's positions through a surprise attack along the Suez Canal, which in Israel is called the Yom Kippur War, and in Egypt the October War. The strangest thing is that in succeeding where Nasser had failed, the new leader was unable to supplant his predecessor in the hearts of the Arab people. He was even ridiculed and insulted, put in political quarantine and so demonised in some quarters that he ended up being assassinated.

It is strange and also highly revealing for anyone seeking to examine the delicate question of legitimacy. A people still living with the shock of a traumatic defeat suddenly find themselves with a new leader who attains, if not an outright victory, at least a more than honourable semi-success. He should have been adulated, lionised, immediately crowned among the great heroes of the nation, yet the exact opposite happened. If Sadat became an icon, it was for Western and not for Arabic opinion, which never identified with him: not before his spectacular trip to Jerusalem in November 1977, and certainly not after. The Arab people never accorded him that instinctive, almost carnal, legitimacy in their hearts, which Nasser, despite his setbacks, faults and defeats, bene-fited from until his death.

There was probably some unconscious resentment of Sadat for having succeeded Nasser, just as one may hate a mother's new partner simply because he has taken the place of a beloved father. In France, for example, all those who held the reins of power after Napoleon suffered in compar-ison with him, especially those who bore the same name. That the reign of the great emperor had been ruinous and ended in defeat and foreign occupation did not matter. People are grateful to whoever offers them an epic, a dream, the admiration of others, and a scrap of pride. The Napoleonic period was the last during which France occupied first rank among the nations of the earth, and during which it tried to unite Europe around it through the combined force of its arms and ideas. Nasser's moment was less ambitious, but by the yardstick of what still seemed possible for the Arabs, it played a similar role, and it remains in people's memories as a moment of glory.

10

Everyone will draw their own lessons from the failure of this venture. Sadat conceived a profound distrust of the Arab lands where his predecessor had constantly got bogged down: the Yemenis, Jordanians, Palestinians, Lebanese, Syrians, Libyans and the rest were all ready to fight, he would mutter to those close to him, 'right to the last Egyptian soldier'.

Reckoning that his country had endured enough without any recompense, he wished to withdraw once and for all from the Arab–Israeli conflict which had exhausted him, and which was damaging his relations with the prosperous West. He would come to think of the Arabs as 'them' rather than 'us'. Perhaps he would not say it overtly, but those with an interest picked up on it. As a result, when Sadat took a decision, the Arabs did not view it as theirs. And if he remained legitimate as Egyptian president, he was not perceived as – nor did he seek to be – the natural leader of the Arab nation.

At the end of his life, many Arabs even placed Sadat firmly among the enemies and the traitors – not just Arabs of nationalist and Islamist persuasion, who were outraged at his reconciliation with the Jewish state, but also a significant proportion of moderate, pro-Western leaders, who resented the fact that he had made any regional peace impossible by withdrawing Israel's principal Arab neighbour from the conflict. Their reasoning went like this: the power relations in the Middle East were already unfavourable to the Arabs. If, in addition, Egypt disengaged from the conflict, the imbalance would be such that Israel would no longer be willing to cede anything at all; not only would the Arabs no longer be able to make war, but they could not even secure an honourable peace. By choosing the path of a separate peace, Sadat made a true regional peace impossible and consigned the Arab world to a permanent state of instability.

It will take historians several more decades to determine with certainty whether the bold initiative by Nasser's successor when he went to Jerusalem, shook hands with Menachim Begin and Moshe Dayan, and addressed the Knesset marked the beginning of a bumpy ride towards a real peace between Israelis and Arabs, or rather the burial of all hope of it.

Abandoned by Sadat, Nasser's pan-Arabic heritage was coveted by many others, especially those to whom the new oil wealth had given the means to realise grand ambitions. Among them were men such as the Libyan leader, Muammar Gaddafi, who came up with numerous projects for union before getting tired of Arab quarrels and turning resolutely to Africa. And men such as the militant Ba'athist Saddam Hussein, who managed to make himself leader of a country that had a large population, great natural riches and a historical stature comparable with that of Egypt, since it was the cradle of several ancient civilisations – the Sumerian,

Akkadian, Assyrian and Babylonian – and seat of the most prestigious of the Arab empires, that of the Abbasids. He too nurtured the ambition to replace Nasser – but he failed, and we know the disastrous ending to that story.

Both these candidates for the role of pan-Arabic leader had come to power in the wake of the 1967 debacle. The Libyan 'Free Officer' presented himself as the Egyptian Free Officer's spiritual heir and promised to help repair the affront; the Iraqi activist meanwhile mocked Nasser and his army's failures, promising to eclipse him with his own military exploits.

Saddam, however, was never viewed by the Arabs as a new Nasser and he never benefited from genuine popular support, either in his own country or in the wider region. And even if many rallied to his support on the two occasions when he was at war with the United States, it was not because they had confidence in him but because they did not want to witness another Arab defeat or experience yet again the shame, humiliation and destruction, nor suffer the whole world's mockery.

The consequence of Saddam Hussein's two defeats was to seal the fate of the political ideology which had dominated the Middle East for almost a century: pan-Arabic nationalism.

It is true that this doctrine had for a time already been holed below the water line. Nasser had taken it to its zenith, and his defeat could only discredit the idea. Sadat was not alone in decreeing that henceforth his own country's national interests would come before those of the wider Arab world. Other leaders – of the Iraqis, Palestinians, Syrians, Jordanians or whoever – who criticised him nonetheless acted in the same way. Each of them had their own country's interests at heart, or those of their regime, clan or simply themselves. In any case, all attempts at union had failed; all that remained of the pan-Arabic idea were hollow slogans which some politicians still used and some die-hards believed in, but they had little influence on real behaviour.

For a time, after the defeat of 1967, salvation was sought in Marxism. This was the time of Che Guevara, the Vietnam War and the export version of Maoism. The Arabs drew comparisons and blamed themselves. One story which did the rounds following the 1967 disaster was about a senior Egyptian official who was furious about what had happened and exploded in front of the Soviet ambassador: 'All the arms you sold us were worthless!' The diplomat simply replied: 'They were the same as we gave to the Vietnamese.'

Whether it is apocryphal or not, the joke sums up the problem well. How come that, with similar arms, one people managed to stand up to the most powerful army in the world, while another was beaten by its tiny neighbour? For some people, the answer was blindingly obvious: traditional nationalism, whether bourgeois or petit-bourgeois, had to be got rid of and replaced with a 'coherent' revolutionary ideology, that of peoples who came out on top. The Arab Nationalist Movement, led by Dr George Habash, officially adopted Marxist-Leninism and the armed struggle, and went on to form the Popular Front for the Liberation of Palestine, a name which contains neither the adjective 'Arab' nor any explicit reference to nationalism. A branch of the same movement managed to gain power in Yemen in 1969 and declare a 'popular democracy'. Almost everywhere throughout the Arab world, from the Gulf to Morocco, intellectuals and political organisations 'Leninised' their credos, their alliances and sometimes simply their language. Some did it out of opportunism, others from sincere conviction because they saw in it a response to Arab defeat and progress in thought beyond social conformism and narrow nationalism. They also saw an alternative future – at least as it was imagined at that time. In fact this brief flirtation with Marxist-Leninism would just be a transitory stage between the era of nationalism and that of the Islamists, a historical parenthesis whose end would leave a bitter after-taste and for many people would contribute to increasing their feelings of discouragement, rage and impotence.

If Communism had simply been defeated by the forces it was fighting, it would probably have secretly spread thereafter as a powerful form of secular messianism. Of course, that was not how things turned out. Before it could be struck down by the 'class enemy', it was already widely discredited. Its approach to the arts was one of severe censorship, its concept of freedom of thought resembled that of the Inquisition, and its exercise of power sometimes brought to mind those Ottoman sultans who, on coming to power, assiduously massacred their brothers and nephews for fear that they might think of challenging them for the throne.

The examples I have in mind are not just of Stalinist purges. I have much more recent memories from the only two countries to have been governed by explicitly Marxist-Leninist movements: South Yemen from 1969 to 1990 and

Afghanistan from 1978 to 1992. In both cases, scores were settled between rival factions with sub-machine guns in the middle of politburo meetings. Was this just a coincidence? Similar events happened in the 1930s, '40s, '50s and '60s, not just in Moscow but also in Prague, Belgrade, Tirana, and in Beijing during the Cultural Revolution, and later in Addis Ababa when Ethiopia was ruled by a communist military junta known as the Derg – not to mention the Khmer Rouge. So was it a coincidence? No, it was routine, a modus operandi, a way of doing things.

I write this with sadness, as in these movements, good people lost their way, people who sincerely wanted to modernise their societies, who advocated the spread of knowledge, education of girls, equality of opportunity, liberation of minds, weakening of tribalism and the end of feudal privileges. Among the ruins of their betrayed hopes in Kabul and elsewhere, plants of quite a different sort were soon to take root.

11

The desire to be fair and concern for historical truth oblige me to add to these charges some others, with different accused.

The Soviets bear the main responsibility for Afghanistan's descent into disorder, but it was the Americans who organised the massacre of the modernising elite in Indonesia. Until the mid-1960s, the world's most populous Muslim nation was home to a Communist Party whose membership numbered nearly one and a half million and which participated in government under the aegis of the nationalist president, Ahmed Sukarno, the architect of independence. Sukarno had established a regime which was secular and authoritarian without being brutal, and he played a prominent role on the international stage; in April 1955, he hosted the Bandung Conference for African and Asian nations, which was the start of the Non-Aligned Movement.

Angered by the nationalisation of Indonesia's mines and Jakarta's links with Beijing and Moscow, the US, which was beginning to get bogged down in the Vietnam War, decided to resort to drastic measures. Its success was total. As a result of a remarkable operation, the details of which only became known decades later, the Communists and the left-wing nationalists were outlawed, rounded up and massacred in large numbers in the universities, civil service, in districts of the capital and even in the remotest villages. The most serious estimates talk of 600,000 deaths between October 1965 and summer 1966. Power was then given to General Suharto, who for over twenty years maintained a dictatorship which was corrupt and obscurantist – but resolutely anti-Communist. When the country emerged from that tunnel, the Indonesian vision of Islam, once reputed to be the most tolerant in the world, was tolerant no longer. The prospects of secularising society had been destroyed – collateral damage in the struggle against the Communist peril.

Some will point out that this happened during the Cold War. Maybe so. But if that excuse is not admissible for Communist crimes in Budapest in 1956, neither is it admissible for anti-Communist crimes in Jakarta in 1966. A crime is a crime, a massacre is a massacre, and the extermination of elites promotes regression.

Moreover, Indonesia is not the only Muslim country in which the leaders who advocated political independence and state control of their principal natural resources were countered with ferocious efficiency by the West. Sometimes this was because they were the allies of the Soviet Union. But the process also happened in reverse. Some countries turned towards Moscow *because* they had to face the animosity of the Western powers, which would not countenance anyone touching 'their' oil, 'their' mines, 'their' sugar or fruit plantations, 'their' Suez or Panama canals, 'their' military bases or 'their' concessions – in other words, their global supremacy.

In the case of Iran, which I have already mentioned, there is no doubt that Dr Mossadegh dreamt only of establishing a modernising pluralist democracy on the Western model. He had no intention of setting up a Marxist-Leninist dictatorship, nor an ultra-nationalist regime, nor any sort of despotism. He was an upright, self-effacing, depressive man, constantly on the point of quitting public life to go and shut himself away in his library, but he was profoundly motivated by injustice and poverty and only wanted the resources of his country to be used for the advancement of his people. It was for that reason alone that he was forced out of power in 1953 in a coup d'état planned and executed by the US and British secret services, as numerous accounts attest (some of them in the form of subsequently published confessions).

It was no coincidence that this betrayal of its own principles by the West resulted a quarter of a century later in the Iranian revolution which founded contemporary political Islam.

In Nasser's day, militant Islamist movements, especially the Muslim Brotherhood, were forced to remain in the shadows on account of the repression they suffered, and also because the Egyptian president's popularity in the Arab world made all his opponents seem like supporters of colonialism and imperialism.

On the eve of the Egyptian revolution, the Brotherhood was well established in various echelons of society, especially the army. They were conducting a bitter struggle against King Faruk, British interference and the Western presence in general. Their influence spread so rapidly that when the Free Officers seized power in July 1952, many observers imagined that this organisation, which had been unknown up to that point, was just a manifestation of the Brotherhood, a façade, perhaps even simply their military wing. We know today that several participants in the coup were indeed linked to the Islamist movement, some intimately and others more informally.

But the principal architect of the coup, Nasser, very soon came to view the Brotherhood as rivals. They were too powerful to be used as a mere instrument in the hands of the Free Officers, and he had no desire to be their puppet. He came into conflict with them, sought ways to undermine their influence, and after they tried to assassinate him in 1954, he had some of their leaders executed and others imprisoned. Those who managed to escape the crack-down fled to Western Europe, the US or Arab countries which opposed Nasser, such as Jordan or Saudi Arabia.

When the Egyptian president nationalised the Suez Canal in 1956 and emerged victorious from his confrontation with the British, French and Israelis, thereby immediately becoming the hero of the Arab masses, the Brotherhood could no longer oppose him openly. Each time they tried to raise their heads, there was another crack-down, as for example in 1966, when their most brilliant intellectual Sayyid Qutb was condemned to death and hanged after a summary trial. Arab public opinion at the time was not much affected because it associated the Islamists with the 'reactionary monarchies' and the Western countries where they had sought refuge.

After the defeat of Nasserism and the painful self-examination which followed, the Islamists were once again able to get a hearing. 'We told you that you shouldn't trust that charmer!' Though their voice was at first hesitant, whispering, half-hidden, it would grow more and more confident, until it became dominant, even deafening.

Everything that had happened in the world during the previous decades helped the Islamists' arguments to prevail in Arab societies. The successive failures of regimes which called themselves Arab nationalist would end up totally discrediting this ideology and giving credibility to those who had always said that the very idea of an Arab nation was a Western import and that the only nation worthy of the name was the nation of Islam. The acceleration of globalisation would increase the need for and credibility of a global ideology which swept aside borders and went beyond local allegiances. For a small fraction of the population that was Marxism; for the vast majority it could only be religion. And in any case the collapse of the Soviet camp would conclude this debate once and for all in favour of the Islamist movements, but without them transforming themselves into parties of government, and without the dilemma of lost legitimacy being resolved.

For one of the major consequences of the successive defeats of Nasser, Saddam and others is that the very idea of an Arab head of state who can stand up to the West, as was the case in the 1950s and '60s, has ceased to be credible. Anyone wishing to remain in power has to make himself acceptable to the superpower, even if, in order to do so, he has to go against the wishes of his people. Those who are radically opposed to the US, whether by arms or violent rhetoric, generally have an interest in staying in the shadows.

And so two parallel political universes developed, one visible but lacking popular support, and the other hidden and possessing a certain popularity, but unable to assume the responsibility of power long-term. Those who represent the former are perceived as native lackeys in the pay of the enemy; those who represent the latter are mere outlaws. Neither of them has true legitimacy; one because they govern without the people, and the other because they are manifestly incapable of governing, as much due to international hostility as to their own political culture, which predisposes them to radical opposition, doctrinal intransigence and the issuing of *fatwas*, rather than the inevitable compromises required to govern a state. This is a dead end which the Islamists in Egypt, Sudan, Algeria, Morocco and Jordan became aware of and which was made abundantly apparent when Hamas won the Palestinian elections.

For any human society, the absence of legitimacy is a form of weightlessness which disturbs all forms of behaviour. When no authority, institution or individual is able to boast true moral credibility, when people come to believe that the world is a jungle in which the survival of the fittest is the universal law, and where any action is permissible, then a drift towards deadly violence, tyranny and chaos becomes inevitable.

As a result, the erosion of legitimacy in the Arab world cannot be treated as a vague topic to be pondered by specialists. One of the lessons of 11 September 2001 is that in this era of globalisation, no type of disorder remains strictly local, and when it affects the emotions, self-image and daily life of hundreds of millions of people, its effects are felt all over the planet.

12

After this long development on the loss of legitimacy in Arab countries, I want to return for a moment to the other crisis of legitimacy which contributes to the disorder of the world: the global role of the United States. I want to underline that the pertinent question for me is not whether US democracy functions properly; I don't know many which function better. But even if it were the most perfect system, even if all citizens of voting age exercised their right to vote in ideal conditions, the problem would remain the same: from the moment at which the votes of US citizens, who make up 5 per cent of the world's population, become more significant for the future of the whole of humanity than those of the remaining 95 per cent, there is something dysfunctional in the way global politics works.

It is as though someone decreed that the inhabitants of Florida alone were going to choose the US president, and the electorate in all the other states of the union would only elect state governors and local authorities. I have again taken Florida as an example as its population happens to represent exactly 5 per cent of the US population.

It is true that there is not too much indignation when the preferences of those who have the privilege of voting elect someone we might have chosen ourselves. But that only masks the anomaly; it does not remove it.

At the beginning of this second part, I wrote that the 'jurisdiction' of the US administration now covered the whole planet. The word was in quotation marks, given that the authority exercised by Washington does not result from a mandate bestowed on it by the world's people. Within the US, it is a *de jure* mandate. In the rest of the world it is a de facto government, with questionable legitimacy.

It is not easy to discuss this question and at the same time firmly reject the systematic anti-Americanism which reached its zenith in the first years of this century. However, that is the line I am sticking to; first out of conviction, given that I feel neither servility nor rancour towards our global 'suzerain'; and also because it is the only way to understand the dramas of our times and seek solutions. I shall therefore set aside the question of whether the US has shown expansionist and hegemonic tendencies since its inception. It is not that this question does not interest me, but it seems superfluous to spend time on it, given all the other countries that have used and abused their power whenever history has granted them the opportunity to do so. Indeed, if the Russians, Japanese, Germans, British or French – to mention only those nations which have dreamed of global hegemony in the course of the past two centuries – had been able to attain a global status comparable to that of the United States, their behaviour would have been even more high-handed. I suspect that it will be the same in the future with China and India.

★   ★   ★

The United States is undoubtedly the beneficiary of the disorder which is visible in the political management of the world's affairs. But it is also a victim of it. Unless it manages to recover, its unhealthy relations with the rest of the world may cause more lasting and far-reaching traumas than those which followed its engagement in Vietnam.

The position it attained at the end of the Cold War – that of the world's only superpower – has been a mixed blessing. Every entity – whether physical or moral – has need of fixed limits. Every power needs a counter-power, to protect others from its excesses, and also to protect it from itself. This is an elementary rule of politics and one of the foundations of American democracy – the intangible principle of checks and balances, by virtue of which no institution can exercise its privileges without having to answer to another institution which serves as a safeguard. And it is also, one might say, a law of nature. Writing this, I am thinking of those children who are born with an insensitivity to pain. As a result of this condition, they are constantly in danger, because they run the risk of injuring themselves very seriously without realising; perhaps they sometimes feel an intoxicating sense of invulnerability, but it is a feeling which leads them to ill-advised behaviour.

Precisely because it has had the feeling of being able to do more or less whatever it wants on the international stage, the world's only superpower has committed errors which it would have avoided during the Cold War.

At the start, the US displayed a desire to convince others that it was right. If it wanted to intervene militarily anywhere other than Central America, it tried to form credible coalitions; when the United Nations demurred, it appealed to Nato, as in the case of the Kosovo conflict, or to significant regional forces, as in the case of the first Gulf War.

The last largely consensual mission was Afghanistan in the autumn of 2001. Thanks to universal antipathy to the Taliban, whose involvement in the attacks of 11 September was obvious, the Americans had no trouble finding allies. But when, fifteen months later, they tried to muster similar support for invading Iraq, they were confronted with a global diplomatic revolt, in which France was the most heeded spokesman, and in which Germany, Russia, China and the vast majority of the other countries in the world took part. This rebellion can in large measure be put down to the behaviour of the Republican administration, which on various issues, notably global warming and the international criminal court, gave the impression of ignoring or sometimes scorning the opinions of the world's other nations. This was an attitude that was already perceptible before the Twin Towers attacks, but it became more pronounced afterwards, as though the aggression which the US had just suffered removed any obligation towards the international community. Moreover, the administration disregarded the reluctance of the UN Security Council and the stormy opposition of world opinion. It concocted a clutch of pretexts and invaded Iraq in March 2003 with its group of remaining allies.

Unsurprisingly, the US army quickly defeated the Iraqis, but its military victory turned immediately into a political and moral defeat whose consequences are unfathomable.

The US, with its culture of transparency – which is without equal in the world – ceaselessly dissects this misadventure in order to perform its autopsy, to understand how it got there and how to avoid the same thing happening again. It now understands better the risks inherent in the solitary exercise of power in such a complex, variegated world as ours. It knows that you must stay attentive to others, listen to all opinions, those of enemies as well as allies, and that you can avoid the hazards and stop yourself before you leap over the final guardrail.

One might also wonder if the same 'insensitivity to pain' which has disordered the behaviour of our sole global suzerain and greatly harmed it in the end has not also damaged our global economic system.

It is true that the market economy has demonstrated its superiority compared to bureaucratic and centrally planned economies, which no one wants to return to, especially the former Communist states. However, in becoming the only model, capitalism has lost a useful and probably irreplaceable critic which used to take it to task for its social failings, and prodded it over workers' rights and inequalities. And even if those rights were less respected in Communist countries than in most capitalist ones, and even if unions were more tightly muzzled, even if the pernicious nomenklatura system made any reference to the principle of equality hollow, the simple fact of having this challenge, these attacks, this rhetoric, this permanent pressure within every society and at global level, obliged capitalism to be more social, less unequal, more attentive to workers and their representatives. This was a

corrective necessary on the ethical and political level and
even ultimately for the efficient and rational running of the
market economy.

Without this corrective, the system rapidly degenerated,
like a shrub that was no longer pruned and returned to a wild
state. Its relation to money and the way in which it is earned
became obscene.

I agree that there is no shame in making money. Nor, I
believe, is there any shame in enjoying the fruits of prosperity.
Our age offers us so many good and beautiful things that it
would be an insult to life to refuse to enjoy them. But should
money be completely disconnected from all production, from
all physical and intellectual effort, all socially useful activity?
Should our stock exchanges turn into giant casinos in which
the fate of millions of people, both rich and poor, are decided
on the throw of a dice? Should our most venerable financial
institutions end up behaving like drunken louts? Should the
savings of a lifetime's effort be wiped out, or multiplied by
thirty, in a matter of seconds according to esoteric processes
which the bankers themselves do not understand at all?

These are serious disturbances, the implications of which
go far beyond the world of finance and the economy.
Because one can legitimately ask, given what is going on,
why people still lead lives of honest work, why a young
person would still want to become a teacher rather than a
drug dealer; and how, in such an environment, ideals and
knowledge can be transmitted, how a minimum of the social
fabric can be preserved so that fragile and essential things
such as freedom, democracy, happiness, progress and civilisation survive.

Is there any need to spell out that this financial disorder is also – and perhaps above all – a symptom of the disorder in our scale of values?

III

Imaginary Certainties

I

The moral crisis of our time is sometimes discussed in terms of a loss of bearings or a loss of meaning. These phrases do not ring true to me, because they give the impression that we have to rediscover those lost bearings, along with forgotten forms of solidarity and discredited types of legitimacy. In my view, it is not a matter of rediscovering but of inventing anew. We cannot face the challenges of a new era by promoting the fantasy of a return to how we used to behave. We shall have woken up to this fact when we recognise that our times are unlike any other: particular relationships exist between people and between human societies; specific tools are at our disposal; and specific challenges have to be confronted.

As far as relations between nations and the management of the planet's resources are concerned, history's record is far from exemplary, littered as it is with devastating wars, crimes against human dignity, massive waste and tragic mistakes – all of which have brought us to our present pass. Rather than embellishing and idealising the past, we need to ditch the reflexes it has taught us, since they have turned out to be disastrous in the modern world. We need to jettison all our prejudices and outdated, atavistic behaviour to embark squarely on a new phase of the human adventure, a phase in which everything must be created from scratch – forms of solidarity, legitimacy, identity, values and reference points.

In order to avoid misunderstanding, let me hasten to make clear that if, from my point of view, the solution does not lie in some outdated return to traditional morals or old forms of legitimacy, nor does it lie in moral relativism, which, in the name of a lazy, vulgar form of modernity, sanctifies supreme selfishness and worships all forms of negation. It wallows in an attitude of 'every man for himself' and ends up with the worst of precepts: *'Après moi, le déluge!'* to which climate change could give a literal meaning.

Both these opposing attitudes lead by convergent paths to the same disorder. We need something quite different today. If we must leave old forms of legitimacy behind, it must be for better forms, not worse. A new scale of values needs to be worked out which will enable us to manage everything better than we have done in the past: our diversity, our environment, our resources, our knowledge, our tools, our power, our balances – in other words, our common future and our capacity for survival. What we do not need is a rejection of every scale of values.

'Values' is a word which is both versatile and debased. It navigates easily between the financial and spiritual spheres, and in the field of beliefs it can be a synonym for progress or conformism, for moral liberation or submission. And so I need to make clear the sense in which I am using it and the beliefs I attach to it, not in order to rally anyone at all to my standard – I do not have one and I keep my distance from parties, factions and cliques, since nothing is more precious to me than freedom of thought – but because it seems honest in setting out my vision to say unambiguously what I believe and how I would like things to end up.

From my point of view, leaving behind the disorder that affects the world for something better requires adopting a scale of values based on the primacy of culture. I would go so far as to say based on salvation through culture.

André Malraux has often had a quotation attributed to him which he probably never said: the twenty-first century 'will be religious or it will not be at all'. I suppose that those final words – 'or it will not be at all' – mean that we will not be able to get our bearings in the maze of modern life without some spiritual compass.

This century is still young, but we already know that religion can lead humanity astray just as easily as its absence can.

That the absence of religion can cause suffering was amply demonstrated in Soviet society. But its abusive presence can also cause suffering; that much was clear in the time of Cicero, or of Averroes, Spinoza or Voltaire, and if the excesses of the French and Russian revolutions, Nazism and some secular tyrannies have tended to make us forget that fact in the last two centuries, there have been plenty of events since then to serve as a reminder. Events which, I hope, have given us a better appreciation of the role religion ought to play in our lives.

I am tempted to say the same thing about Mammon. Inveighing against material wealth and blaming those who strive to acquire it is a futile pursuit which has always served as a pretext for the worst sort of demagoguery. But making money the touchstone of all respectability, the basis for all power and all hierarchies, results in the social fabric unravelling.

Humanity has experienced so many contradictory trends in the space of two or three generations: communism/capitalism; atheism/religion. Should we resign ourselves to these pendulum swings and the disorder which results from them? Once bitten, should we not try to learn from our experiences and want in the end to escape these demoralising dilemmas?

It may seem a little too predictable for a writer, or indeed anyone in the cultural sphere, to advocate a scale of values based on culture. It may even provoke a smile. But that is because of a misunderstanding of the term.

The view of culture as just one field among many or a way of making life more pleasurable for a certain sort of person is a century or even a millennium out of date. Today the role of culture is nothing less than to provide us with the intellectual and moral tools for survival.

How are we to fill the extra decades that modern medicine has given us? More and more of us are living longer and better lives, but are inevitably prey to boredom, haunted by a sense of emptiness, and inevitably tempted to escape by indulging in an orgy of consumerism. If we do not want to exhaust the planet's resources very quickly, we shall have to prioritise other forms of satisfaction as soon as possible, other sources of pleasure, in particular the acquisition of knowledge and the development of a flourishing inner life.

This is not a matter of imposing self-denial or becoming an ascetic. I for one am a fervent epicurean and prohibitions of any kind irritate me. We will continue very happily to use the fruits of the earth – and often to abuse them – and I will not be the one to cast the first stone. But if we want to benefit fully in the long term from what life can offer, we are going to have to alter our behaviour. Not to reduce our range of sensations, but on the contrary to enlarge and enhance it and to look for other satisfactions which may turn out to be yet more intense.

We already distinguish when it comes to energy sources between fossil fuels, which are finite and polluting, and renewable sources, such as solar, wind and geothermal, which are not. We could introduce a similar distinction when it comes to our lifestyles. We could seek to satisfy our needs and desires through consuming more, which would take its toll on the planet's resources and cause destructive tensions. But equally, we could satisfy them in other ways, by giving priority to lifelong learning and by encouraging people to study languages, to become passionate about artistic disciplines, to become familiar with various sciences so that they are able to appreciate the significance of discoveries in biology or astrophysics. Knowledge is a universe without limits; all of us can draw upon it unrestrainedly throughout our lives and it will never run out. And even better, the more we draw on knowledge, the less we will deplete the planet.

This is already reason enough to consider the primacy of culture as a discipline for survival. But that is not the only reason. There is another, just as fundamental and which would in itself justify putting culture at the heart of our scale of values: it is the way in which it can help us handle human diversity.

Will people from diverse backgrounds who live side by side in the world's cities and countries forever look at each other through the distorting lenses of received opinion, age-old prejudice and crude stereotypes? It strikes me that the time has come to change our habits and priorities, and to listen more seriously to the world we share – because there are no longer any strangers in this century; there are only travelling companions. Whether our fellow humans live across the street or on the other side of the world, they are only a short step away; our behaviour affects them intimately as their behaviour affects us.

If we wish to preserve peace in our societies, towns and neighbourhoods and all over the planet, if we want human diversity to translate into harmonious coexistence rather than tensions which breed violence, it is no longer enough to know others in an approximate, superficial, crude way. We need to know them subtly, up close; I would go as far as to say intimately. And that can only be achieved through their culture. The heart of a people is its literature. That is where it reveals its passions, aspirations, dreams, frustrations, beliefs, its vision of the world around, its perceptions of itself and others – including us. Because when we speak of others we must never lose sight of the fact that, whoever and wherever we may be, we are also 'others' for the rest of the world.

Of course, no one can know all they would like or ought to know about others. There are so many peoples, cultures, languages, and visual, musical, choreographic, theatrical, artisanal and culinary traditions. But if everyone were encouraged to become passionate from childhood and remain so throughout their life about a culture other than their own, for a language freely chosen through personal affinity – and if they studied it more intensively even than they studied the indispensable English language – the result would be a closely woven cultural web covering the whole planet, encouraging threatened identities, reducing hatred, gradually reinforcing belief in the unity of the human adventure and as a result making possible the step change that might save us.

I can see no more crucial objective for this century and it is clear that, in order to achieve it, we must give culture and education the prime place which is their due.

In the US and elsewhere, a sinister era in which it was thought good form to despise culture and to make a lack of culture a proof of authenticity may be coming to an end. This populist attitude paradoxically has something in common with elitism, since both accept that the general public have limited capacities, that you must not make too great intellectual demands of them, that it is enough to give them full shopping trolleys, simplistic slogans and facile amusements in order for them to remain blissfully happy, docile and grateful.

This attitude is contemptuous of democracy and therefore dangerous. Because it is not possible to be fully a citizen or a responsible voter if you passively allow yourself to be manipulated by propagandists, or to be stirred up or calmed down according to the whim of your leaders, or let yourself be docilely led into war. In order to make properly informed decisions, especially in a country whose direction largely determines the fate of the planet, a citizen needs to know the world around him in depth and in detail. To make do with ignorance is a denial of democracy and reduces it to a sham.

For all of these reasons and some others, I believe that our scale of values today can only be based on the primacy of culture and education. And that the twenty-first century – to echo the quotation I cited earlier – will be saved by culture or it will not be at all.

My conviction is not based on any pre-existing doctrine, just on my reading of the events of my time. But I am not insensitive to the fact that the great religious traditions with which I come into contact contain similar exhortations. 'The ink of the sage is worth more than the blood of the martyr,' said the Prophet of Islam. He is also reported as saying: 'The sages are the heirs of the Prophet'; 'Seek knowledge, even in China if you must'; and, 'Study from the cradle to the grave!'

In the Talmud, there is this strong, moving idea: 'The world is only supported by the breath of children studying.'

The struggle to 'support the world' will be hard, but the deluge is not a foregone conclusion. The future is not written in advance; it is up to us to write it, to conceive and build it – and build it with boldness, because we must dare to break with centuries-old habits; with generosity of spirit, because we must assemble, reassure, listen, include and share; above all with wisdom. This is the task which is incumbent on all of us, men and women of all origins; there is no choice but to take it on.

When a country is plunged into chaos, emigration is always an option. When the whole planet is threatened, we cannot go and live elsewhere. If we do not wish to resign ourselves to decline, for ourselves and the generations to come, we must try to influence the outcome of things.

2

Will it be possible in the years ahead to construct a new form of solidarity among people which goes beyond all borders – one that is universal, complex, subtle, thoughtful and adult? One that is independent of religion without in any way being anti-religious or insensitive to people's spiritual needs, which are as real as their physical ones? A solidarity that can transcend nations, communities, ethnicities, without abolishing the abundance of cultures? Which is able to bring people together in the face of the dangers that threaten them, without indulging in apocalyptic rhetoric?

In other words, will we see the emergence in the course of this century of a new, mobilising form of humanism which will not be hostage to any tradition, nor fall into the errors of Marxism, nor appear as the political or ideological tool of the West? For the moment I can see no sign of it. What I do detect is the extraordinary mobilising force of hereditary allegiances which accompany humans from cradle to grave; which they sometimes lose but almost always end up regaining as though they had constantly been held on the end of an invisible leash; which cross the centuries, adapting somehow or other to the changing world, but without ever

losing their hold. And conversely I also see the fragile, transitory, superficial character of the forms of solidarity which try
to transcend these allegiances.

When Marx referred to religion as the 'opium of the people',
he did not do so with mockery or disdain as his disciples often
did. It is perhaps useful to quote the phrase in context: 'Religion
is the sigh of the oppressed creature, the heart of a heartless
world, and the soul of soulless conditions. It is the opium of the
people.' From his point of view, this 'illusory happiness' had to
be abolished so that people would work to build genuine
happiness. From this one might reasonably deduce with hindsight that if the promised happiness turned out to be yet more
illusory, people would return to their consoling opium.

Consequently, it seems to me that if Marx had been able
to witness this resurgence of religion in the political and
social spheres, it would have pained him but not really
surprised him.

Political Islamism prevailed in Arab and Muslim societies at
the expense of nationalism and Marxism, but it was not
content to defeat these doctrines; it assimilated and appropriated them.

The most eloquent example of this was the Iranian revolution of 1979 – a religious event certainly, but also a
nationalist, anti-monarchist, anti-Western, anti-Israeli one,
launched in the name of the impoverished masses. It was a
heady brew which exerted a determining influence on the
whole Muslim world.

Some Muslim leaders had already attempted to weave
together the three strands – national, religious and social.

Among them was President Sukarno of Indonesia, who declared the principle of 'Nasacom', an acronym in the local language for nationalism–religion–communism. But all it amounted to was an artificial amalgam which quickly came unstuck.

Even when communism was replaced by socialism, to avoid too obvious a contradiction with Islam, the combination did not work. Nowhere in the Muslim world did nationalism succeed in assimilating religion the way that religion would assimilate nationalism. When the Turks and the Arabs, after four centuries of coexistence in the Ottoman empire, went their separate ways during the First World War, each of them developing their own brand of nationalism, they were both unmarked by the Islam that united them – in Turkey this was radical under Atatürk's aegis, out of a desire to set a new course, while in the Arab world it was less clear cut, but in the rhetoric, the phrase 'Muslim nation' was discreetly but systematically replaced by 'the Arab nation'. Their respective styles were very different, but the basic assumption was the same: nationalism, which was a new idea, could not use religion as a crutch without losing out.

Of course, ambiguities have always existed. In the eyes of the masses, Nasser was always a hero of Islam. But he avoided making explicit reference to religion, and was careful not to justify his political actions with quotations from the Qur'an because he knew that would mean entering territory where his political enemies, the Muslim Brotherhood, had the upper hand. He never boasted of being a religious president, as his successor Sadat did. Sadat was much less prudent in this regard. In order to free himself from the grip of the Nasserists and tackle the progress made by the left, he sought the support of the Islamists and tried to appropriate their language. But he could not handle the forces he had unleashed for long before they turned on him ferociously.

If religion has never been dissolved in nationalism and still less socialism, the opposite is not the case. Given that nationalist struggles – by the Egyptians, Algerians, Iranians, Chechens and Palestinians – have essentially pitted Muslims against Christian or Jewish adversaries, they could be conducted more easily in the name of a religious community than a linguistic one. And given that the attraction of socialism for the masses resides in its promise to reduce the gulf between the rich and poor, such an objective translates perfectly into religious terms. Islam, like Christianity, has always known how to speak to the poor and draw them in. Everything in nationalism and socialism that was specific, irreducible and indissoluble would be pushed aside or else fall by the wayside by itself; everything that was permanent and substantial would be integrated into a sort of total ideology, at once nationalist and globalist, which claimed to respond to all of humanity's needs, whether spiritual, material or concerned with identity. It became a combat ideology which attracted all those who a few decades earlier would have gravitated towards Nasserism or even communism.

With the exception of the Christian community, which was able to identify with Arab nationalism and Marxism in the past but cannot now identify with an Islamism which excludes them, all those who held defeated doctrines have been able to make their political conversion without too strong a feeling of self-betrayal. Their struggle remains the same against the perennial enemy with the ideological arms of the moment.

Why would someone have declared himself a Maoist, Guevarist or Leninist in the past? Because he wanted to fight effectively against 'American imperialism'. Today, he pursues the same objective in the name of Islam; what's more, he is in step with the people of his neighbourhood, whereas in the past he felt isolated with his leaflets translated from Russian or Little Red Books which no one wanted to read. Hadn't he shouted himself hoarse repeating to young recruits that a revolutionary had to be 'like a fish in water'? Since he started attending the mosque, that is exactly how he feels. He is no longer looked upon as a heathen trying to sell suspect goods manufactured who knows where. Now he speaks a language that everyone understands. Everyone who lives around him, young and old, knows the same verses from the same book.

It used to be very difficult getting people to accept the ability to quote from Lenin, Engels, Lin Biao, Plekhanov, Gramsci or Althusser as a sign of worth. How comforting it now is to be able to tell them that nothing that has been written or thought or invented over the centuries has as much importance as what they themselves already memorised in childhood.

What could be more powerful than a doctrine which also functions as a form of belonging? There is no need even to apply to join – belonging is a birthright, by the grace of the Creator, for ever and ever.

★   ★   ★

What is true of Islam also holds good for other religions. For several decades, Russia gave the impression that Communism was deep-rooted and the Orthodox faith just a frail survivor. But before the end of the last century, Communism was discarded like an unsuccessful graft and the country's new leaders began going to church again.

Whether this is a cause for rejoicing or regret – and I will not conceal the fact that I do not find it particularly reassuring – it must be admitted that religious allegiances, which are passed on spontaneously from one generation to the next without the need to belong or even to believe, are much more durable than acquired beliefs. France may have stopped thinking of itself as a Catholic country a long time ago, and in fact, faith, religious practice and moral precepts it could hardly be said to be one. But it remains so in its cultural identity, just as Stalin's Russia remained Orthodox and Atatürk's Turkey Muslim.

This paradox is illustrated by an old Jewish story about a father who was an atheist and wanted to give his son the best possible education, and therefore sent him to the Jesuits. Despite his background, the child had to attend catechism classes in which he was taught the Catholic doctrine of the Trinity. When he got home, he asked his father if it was true that there are three Gods. His father frowned and said: 'Listen to me, son. There is only one God and we don't believe in him.'

A major lesson from the last century is that ideologies come and go but religions remain. Not so much the beliefs but the sense of belonging; although beliefs can be reconstructed on the foundation of that sense of belonging.

What makes religions virtually indestructible is that they offer their members a durable anchor for their identity. At other times in history, other newer, more 'modern' types of solidarity, such as class and nation, have seemed to be in the ascendant. But up to now it is religion which has had the last word. It was thought that it could be banished from the public sphere and confined within the borders of worship. It turned out to be difficult to confine and tame, and impossible to uproot. Those who consigned it to the history museums found themselves prematurely relegated there. Meanwhile, religion revealed itself as prosperous, and capable of conquering and often even of invading – everywhere, and especially in Islamic countries.

3

The very close proximity between Islam and politics is worth pondering, as it is one of the most troubling and puzzling aspects of the contemporary world.

Strangely, this phenomenon is explained in the same way by both supporters of religious radicalism and critics of Islam; the former because it is their creed and the latter because it fits with their prejudices. All agree that Islam and politics are inseparable, that it has always been thus, that it is written in the holy texts, and that it is futile to want to change it. This opinion, which is sometimes loudly proclaimed and is always implicit, is the subject of such a consensus that it possesses all the trappings of truth.

I have my doubts. If it were just a matter of the critical evaluation of a religion, its practices and beliefs, I would not spend much time on it. Although I have always lived in close proximity to Islam, I am not a specialist on the Muslim world, still less an Islamic scholar. I cannot be counted on if you are seeking to know 'what Islam really says'. Nor should I be counted on to write that all religions preach harmony. My profound belief is that all doctrines, whether religious or secular, have within them the seeds of dogmatism and intolerance. In some individuals these seeds germinate, and in others they remain dormant.

I readily admit that I have no more idea than the next man about what Christianity, Islam, Judaism and Buddhism 'really say'. I believe that every faith is open to an infinite number of interpretations, which depend much more on the historical trajectory of human societies than holy texts. At every stage of history, the texts say what people want to hear. Some words are suddenly illuminated which were yesterday invisible. Others, which once seemed essential, fall into oblivion. The same scriptures which used to justify the divine right of kings now accommodate democracy. And just ten lines on from a verse in praise of peace it is easy to find another which celebrates war. Every passage in the Old and New Testaments and in the Qur'an has given rise to countless readings, and it would be absurd for anyone to assert after so many centuries of interpretation and controversy that each has only one possible meaning.

I understand why the zealots do assert this; it is their role. It is difficult to stick to a particular reading of the text if you think that other interpretations are equally valid. But the observer of history, whether a believer or not, cannot take that position. From his point of view, it is not a matter of determining which interpretation of the Scriptures is compatible with the teaching of the faith, but of evaluating the influence of doctrines on the course of the world; and also conversely the influence of the course of the world on doctrines.

I find the current opinion on the relationship between Islam and politics worrying because it constitutes the mental foundation of the 'clash of civilisations' which has made the world a violent place and threatens all our futures. From the point at which religion and politics in Islam are deemed to be indissolubly linked and it is accepted that this constitutes an immutable given written in the holy texts, the idea that this clash will never end – not in thirty years, nor in fifty, nor a hundred and fifty, nor a thousand – becomes established, as does the notion that we are in the presence of two distinct forms of humanity. This is an idea that I find demoralising, of course, and destructive, but above all simplistic, inexact and ill-considered.

When the acts of violence committed by the US military in Abu Ghraib were revealed, one of the published photos showed a naked detainee forced to walk on all fours with a rope around his neck, held on a leash by a triumphantly smiling female soldier. Invited to comment on a US television channel, a Middle East specialist explained to viewers that in order to understand the horror aroused by these images in the Muslim world, you had to know that in Islam the dog is considered an unclean animal.

I was speechless. Did that mean that if an Irish or Australian detainee had been forced onto all fours with a rope around his neck and made to walk naked in the corridors of the prison, he wouldn't have had anything to object to as dogs are not considered unclean in Ireland or Australia?

What's more, this opinion was expressed by a brave, honest academic who has constantly campaigned against the war in Iraq. In this interview, he was ingenuously trying to denounce the acts of violence committed by some of his compatriots. So what is at issue here is not his intention, but the way of thinking which he unconsciously transmitted and which consists in treating Islam as though it came from a different planet.

I do not doubt that there are important specific characteristics in the journey the Muslim world has taken, and especially in the relationship it has established between religion and politics. But they vary greatly from one country to another and from one era to another; they result from the complicated history of peoples rather than the application of a doctrine; and they are not always to be found where we expect them.

And so, contrary to appearances, one of the tragedies of the Muslim world, both in the past and today, is that politics has constantly impinged upon the religious domain – and not the other way round. From my point of view, this is due not to the content of the faith but to factors which could be termed institutional, and principally to the fact that Islam has not favoured the emergence of a centralised 'church'. It strikes me that if an institution similar to the papacy had been able to prevail, things would probably have happened differently.

I suppose that no one would claim that the popes have historically been promoters of freedom of thought, social advancement or political rights. And yet they have been – indirectly and by reaction against them, but nevertheless in a powerful way. By being a counterweight to holders of temporal power, they constantly limited the arbitrary exercise of royal power and quashed imperial arrogance, and in so doing preserved a sort of breathing space. It was in the gaps between two forms of absolutism – papal and royal – that the embryonic modernity of the future slowly took shape, a modernity which would one day shake the thrones of Europe and the authority of sovereign popes.

Moreover, the Christian and Muslim worlds sometimes experienced comparable phenomena at the same moment. Just as there was a duality between emperors and popes, so too was there a duality between sultans and caliphs. In both cases, rulers with political authority and military power presented themselves as protectors of the faith, while pontiffs with spiritual authority tried hard to preserve their autonomy, their sphere of influence and the dignity of their office. In both cases, conflicts were frequent, and similar incidents occurred in Rome and Baghdad between the tenth and thirteenth centuries, when powerful monarchs feigned humble repentance at the feet of the man of God, but all the while were preparing revenge.

The difference is that Saint Peter's successors managed to hold on to their throne while the Prophet's did not. Confronted with the political and military power of the sultans, the caliphs faced one defeat after another, were stripped of their prerogatives and eventually lost all autonomy of action. One day in the sixteenth century, the Ottoman sultan quite simply appropriated the title of caliph, which he added to his other pompous titles and retained until Kemal Atatürk decided to separate the two roles again in November 1922. Sixteen months later, he abolished the institution of caliph with a stroke of his pen. The last caliph, Abdul Mejid, a talented painter who exhibited his work in various European capitals, died in exile in Paris in 1944.

Within Western Christianity, meanwhile, the popes remained powerful. In France, the fight to prevent the encroachment of religious authority in the political sphere was intense; until the early twentieth century, in fact, Rome condemned the very idea of the republic. Many Catholics viewed it as an impious regime, and when the opportunity presented itself in 1940, some of Marshal Pétain's supporters were eager to do away with 'the strumpet'.

In Islam, the problem was always the opposite: not the encroachment of religious authority on the political sphere, but the stifling of religious authority by political authority. And paradoxically, it is because of this, and because of the crushing predominance of the political, that religion spread through the body politic.

4

What ensured that the papacy endured – and what the caliphate so desperately lacked – was a church and a clergy.

Rome was always able to mobilise its tight network of bishops, priests and monks, which covered every kingdom and province right down to the very smallest hamlet on Christian soil. They formed a powerful force, albeit 'soft power', which no monarch could overlook. The ruling pontiff also had the power to excommunicate or to threaten to do so, which in the Middle Ages was a formidable instrument that made emperors tremble just as much as the simple faithful. Islam had none of these things – no church, no clergy and no threat of excommunication. From the start, Islam developed a great distrust of intermediaries, whether saints or confessors. Man is supposed to be in direct dialogue with his Creator, speak only to Him, and be judged by Him alone. Some historians have compared this attitude to Luther's Reformation and there are certainly similarities. Logically, this stance should have encouraged the early emergence of lay societies in the Islamic world. But history never advances in a predictable direction. No one could have foreseen that the enormous power of the papacy would one day end with the reduction of the place of religion in Catholic societies, while the distinctly anti-clerical sensibility of Islam, by preventing the emergence of a strong ecclesiastical institution, would favour an explosion of religion within Muslim societies.

Confronted with sultans, viziers and military commanders, the caliphs found themselves utterly helpless. They were unable to maintain the religious counter-power which was so useful to popes. As a result, princes exercised arbitrary power without restraint. The relatively free space in which embryonic modernity could grow never existed, or certainly not for long enough to allow cities and citizens to flourish.

But the papacy did not limit its influence to that of a counterweight to secular power. As official guardian of orthodoxy, it contributed to maintaining the intellectual stability of Catholic societies and even their overall stability. The lack of a similar institution in the Muslim world was conspicuous every time it was necessary to confront a rebellion that claimed religious legitimacy.

When radical ideas like those of the monk Savonarola in fifteenth-century Florence began to spread, Rome opposed them and its authority allowed it to put an end to them once and for all: the unfortunate Savonarola ended up being burned at the stake. Closer to our own time, and in a different vein, when Catholics in Latin America were tempted in the 1960s by liberation theology and some Colombian priests such as Camilo Torres found themselves under arms alongside Marxists, the church firmly stamped this out. I am not going to discuss the content of this theology, any more than

I am going to consider Savonarola's; what strikes me as significant is how efficiently the papacy cut short any such excesses.

In the Muslim world, a would-be Savonarola or Camilo Torres could not have been checked in the same way. In the absence of a muscular ecclesiastical authority with recognised legitimacy, the most radical ideas regularly spread among the faithful and could not be contained. Today as in the past, any social or political challenge can make free use of religion to attack the established order. Religious leaders in different Muslim countries are generally unable to oppose it, since they are appointed by those in power and are therefore literally in their pay, and consequently have only limited moral credibility.

In my view, it is the absence of a papal-style institution capable of drawing a line between the political and religious which explains the drift that affects the Muslim world, rather than a 'divine directive' creating confusion between the two spheres.

One might wonder if it doesn't come to the same thing, but I don't think so. At least not if we still have hopes of a future for humanity.

It is not unimportant to understand whether this lack of separation between politics and religion results from unchanging dogma or the contingencies of history. For those, like me, who persist in trying to find a way out of the global impasse we have got ourselves stuck in today, it is important to underline that the difference between the trajectories of the two 'rival' civilisations was determined not by an immutable celestial injunction but by human behaviour which can change, and by the historical course of human institutions.

All these institutions are human (I use that adjective purely descriptively, without making any assumptions about their spiritual function). The papacy was not established by the Gospels: there is no mention in them of a sovereign pontiff, of course, given that the title belonged to a pagan dignitary. Likewise, the caliphate was not established by the Qur'an, in which just two men are explicitly referred to by the term 'caliph' (meaning 'heir' or 'successor'). The first of these was Adam, to whom God announced that he was giving the earth – and it is clear from the context that the world was thus being entrusted to the whole of humanity. The second was a historical figure to whom the Creator addressed these severe words: 'I have named you caliph on this earth so that you govern with justice; do not allow yourself to be guided by your passions, which will lead you from the way of God. Those who depart from it will suffer a terrible punishment for having forgotten Judgement Day.' The 'caliph' addressed thus was none other than King David.

Another paradoxical aspect of the papacy is that this eminently conservative institution has allowed progress to be maintained.

I shall illustrate this with an example which may appear trivial: when I was a child, a Catholic woman could not go to mass without covering her head and shoulders. Things had always been thus, and no believer, whether a serving girl or a queen, was allowed to transgress the rule, which the priests applied with zeal and sometimes humour. That makes me recall the priest who approached one of his flock and gave her an apple. When the young woman expressed surprise, he told her that it was only after tasting the apple that Eve realised that she was naked.

The poor woman was certainly not naked; all she had done was wear her long hair down, but clothing requirements could not be broken – until the moment in the early 1960s when the Vatican decided that henceforth women were allowed to attend church without a veil. I suppose that some people must have been irritated or even outraged by a decision that ran counter to an ancient tradition dating all the way back to Saint Paul. He had after all written in his first epistle to the Corinthians:

> For a man indeed ought not to cover his head, forasmuch as he is the image and glory of God; but the woman is the glory of the man. For the man is not of the woman; but the woman of the man. Neither was the man created for the woman; but the woman for the man. For this cause ought the woman to have power on her head because of the angels.

Nonetheless, overnight these words from another age were deemed obsolete; no one tried to insist that Catholic women cover their heads, and it is reasonable to suppose that this advance will not be called into question.

Let me repeat because this is the point I want to make: the popes may have restrained any relaxation of the rule on clothing for nineteen centuries, but from the moment when they judged that this position no longer had any justification, from the moment when they finally took stock of how attitudes had changed, they proceeded to validate the change, so to speak, rendering it virtually irreversible.

In the history of the West, the institution of the church has often functioned in this way, contributing to the material and moral advance of European civilisation, and yet all the while attempting to restrain it. Whether in the domain of science, economics, politics or social behaviour, and especially in matters of sexuality, the papacy's attitude has followed the same course. At the start, the church digs in, applies the brakes, fulminates, threatens, condemns and forbids. Then, after time (sometimes centuries) has passed, it reviews, re-examines and moderates its position. Next, with some reluctance, it accommodates itself to the verdict of human societies. The change is validated – codified, in a manner of speaking, on the register of permitted behaviour. From that moment on, there is no further tolerance of zealots who might wish to reverse things.

For centuries, the Catholic church refused to believe that the earth was round and orbited the sun. And, when it came to the origin of species, it initially condemned Darwin and evolution. Today, it would crack down on any of its bishops who interpreted the holy texts in too literal a manner, as some Arabic *ulemas* and American evangelists do.

The prevailing mistrust in the Muslim tradition, as in the Protestant one, of a centralising religious authority is perfectly legitimate and thoroughly democratic in its inspiration, but it has a disastrous side-effect: without that intolerable central-ising authority, no progress can be irrevocably recorded.

Even when believers have lived their faith for decades in the most generous, enlightened, tolerant fashion possible, they are never completely beyond risk of a 'relapse', never shielded from some zealous interpretation coming along to sweep away their gains. Again – whether in the domain of science, economics, politics or social behaviour – something a benevolent *fatwa* authorised yesterday, a mean-spirited *fatwa* can forbid today with extreme rigour. The same controversies come up again and again over what is and is not permitted, and what is pious and what impious. Without a supreme authority, no advance is definitively validated, and no opinion expressed in past centuries is definitively marked as obsolete. For every step forward there is a step back, so much so that it becomes impossible to tell what is forward and what is back. The door is perpetually open to all forms of escalation, extremism and regression.

Regression is also the word that comes to mind when I read that some US schools which used to offer a rational education have suddenly begun to teach the next generation that the world was created six thousand years ago – on 22 October 4004 BCE, to be precise – and that if fossils are found on earth which seem to date from hundreds of millions of years ago, that is because God aged them through some miracle and placed them there to test the strength of our faith.

In general, strange and worrying beliefs are on the rise, which blithely announce the end of the world and even work to hasten it. These trends probably only affect a small proportion of Christians, some tens of millions of people. But the influence of that minority is not insignificant, given that it is situated in the United States and its members assiduously frequent the corridors of power, sometimes managing to influence the behaviour of the world's sole superpower.

There are a thousand other things I could say, a thousand eloquent examples, to illustrate the impact of institutional, cultural, national or more generally historical factors on the comparative evolution of the two civilisations to which I belong – and the lack of impact of properly doctrinal differences.

My profound conviction is that too much weight is placed on the influence of religion on people, and too little on the influence of people on religion. From the moment in the fourth century when the Roman empire became Christian, Christianity became Roman – abundantly so. It is this historical circumstance which explains the emergence of a sovereign papacy. Taking a wider view, if Christianity contributed to making Europe what it became, Europe also contributed to making Christianity what it became. The two pillars of Western civilisation – Roman law and Athenian democracy – both pre-date Christianity.

Similar observations could be made about Islam and also about non-religious doctrines. If Communism influenced the history of Russia and China, those two countries also determined the history of Communism, whose destiny would have been very different if it had instead triumphed in Germany or England. Foundational texts, whether they are sacred or profane, lend themselves to the most contradictory readings. Hearing Deng Xiaoping claim that privatisation was in direct line with Marxist thought and that the successes of his economic reform demonstrated the superiority of socialism over capitalism may provoke smiles. But this interpretation is no more laughable than any other. In fact, it is certainly more in keeping with the dreams of the author of *Das Kapital* than the delirium of a Stalin, Kim Il-Sung, Pol Pot or Mao Tse-tung.

No one can deny, in any case, seeing the Chinese experiment unfold, that one of the most surprising successes in the history of global capitalism has happened under the aegis of a Communist Party. Is that not a powerful illustration of the malleability of doctrines and the infinite ability of people to interpret them any way they like?

To return to the Muslim world: if we try to understand the political behaviour of those who claim religious legitimacy and wish to change it, we will not identify the problem by searching holy texts, nor will the texts provide an answer. Hastily explaining everything that happens in different Muslim societies through the 'particularity' of Islam is to indulge in platitudes and condemn oneself to ignorance and impotence.

5

For anyone attempting to understand contemporary reality, the notion that religions, ethnic identities and cultures are unique is a useful one, but it requires careful handling. If you disregard it, you will miss its subtleties; if you accord it too much importance, you will fail to grasp the essential.

Today, uniqueness is also an ambiguous notion. Was apartheid not expressly founded on 'respect for the uniqueness' of the blacks? Each of South Africa's populations was supposed to follow the path its own culture destined it for, according to whether it was of European or African origin. Some were supposed to advance towards modernity, while others were supposed to be limited to their ancestral traditions.

The example of South Africa may appear outdated and caricatured. Unfortunately it isn't. The spirit of apartheid is ubiquitous in the world today and is spreading all the time. Sometimes it is spread maliciously and sometimes with the best of intentions.

Perhaps I can illustrate this by recounting an incident which happened in Amsterdam at the beginning of this century. A young woman of Algerian origin went to the town hall with a project that was close to her heart: a club for immigrant women in her neighbourhood, which would enable them to meet each other, get out of the close family environment for a while, relax in a *hamam* and talk openly about their problems. A council official met her, listened and took notes. She asked her to come back a few weeks later to find out whether the council could help her. The young women went off feeling confident. When she returned on the specified date, she was told that unfortunately the project could not go ahead. 'We consulted your local imam and he said that it wouldn't be a good idea. Sorry!'

I believe that the civil servant who said this would not have thought she was promoting segregation, but rather was being eminently respectful. Was it not appropriate to leave it up to the 'tribal chief' to decide what should happen in an ethnic community? An ingenuous question comes to mind: if the young woman who presented the project had been European, would they have left the decision in the hands of her parish priest or pastor? Of course not. And why not?, one might ask equally ingenuously. The responses will inevitably be awkward. The answer lies in what is unspoken but under-stood, and in preconceptions about ethnicity. To put it bluntly, we act like this because 'those people' are not like 'us'. You would have to be completely insensitive not to grasp that this 'respect' for the Other is a form of contempt and a sign of hatred. That at least is how those who are 'respected' experience it.

All human societies since the dawn of time have been affected by the tendency to consider others only in terms of their religious or ethnic differences. It is a way of thinking that sends people from elsewhere back to their traditional allegiances, a mental failing which prevents seeing beyond someone's colour, their accent or their name. But in today's 'global village', such an attitude is no longer tolerable because it compromises the chances of coexistence in every town and every country, and leads to irreparable rifts and a violent future for the whole of humanity.

So what should be done? Pretend not to see differences? Act as if everyone is the same colour and has the same culture and beliefs?

These are reasonable questions and worth pondering for a moment.

We live in a period in which everyone feels obliged to fly a flag declaring their allegiances and to show that they have seen the flags of those they encounter. I do not know if this constitutes a liberation or an abnegation of the self, a form of contemporary politeness or bad manners. It probably depends on the circumstances and the way it is done. But the dilemma is real nonetheless. Pretending not to notice differences between the sexes, in skin colour, accents and the sound of a name, sometimes amounts to concealing and perpetuating centuries-old injustices. On the other hand, systematically and explicitly taking account of distinctive characteristics contributes to locking people into their inherited allegiances and confining them to their respective 'clans'.

A wiser response seems to me to lie in a subtler, more acute and less lazy approach. It is not a matter of ignoring the differences there might be between a Dutch and an Algerian person – to stay with the same example – but, having noted them, of taking time to go beyond these differences, remembering that not all Dutch people are the same, nor all Algerians. A Dutch person may be a believer or an agnostic, enlightened or foolish, on the right or the left, cultivated or uncultivated, hard-working or lazy, honest or a scoundrel, miserable or fun-loving, generous or mean – and the same goes for an Algerian.

Pretending to ignore physical or cultural differences would be absurd, but it would be missing something essential if one limited oneself to the most obvious differences instead of going further towards the person himself as an individual.

Respecting someone means addressing him or her as a whole human being, as a free adult, not as a dependent being who belongs to his community like a serf to the land.

Respecting the Algerian woman would have meant respecting the individual who had devised a project and had the courage to go and present it to the authorities. Rather than dragging her back under the rule of her community leader.

I chose something which happened in Amsterdam as an example on purpose. Ever since the seventeenth century, Amsterdam has been a city which has played a pioneering role in Europe's slow march towards religious tolerance. And I believe that the town hall official who consulted the local imam thought she was acting in complete accord with the spirit of openness which has always characterised the city.

That, after all, was the way that tolerance worked four centuries ago. Religious minorities were authorised to practise their faith freely. And if a member of one of these communities behaved in a reprehensible way, he was firmly brought back into line by his own community leaders. That is how Spinoza came to be excommunicated by his fellow Jews in 1656, when his supposed atheism threatened to compromise relations with their Christian fellow citizens. The question was made all the more sensitive as many Jews, including Spinoza's own father, had arrived in Amsterdam relatively recently after their expulsion from the Iberian peninsula, and did not want to be suspected of behaving disloyally to their hosts, who, given the period, had behaved with unusual magnanimity.

Today's realities are different and infinitely more complex, and attitudes do not have the same meaning. In our epoch, which is menaced by a drift towards global communitarianism, yoking men and women to their religious communities makes problems worse rather than better. Yet that is what numerous European countries do when they encourage immigrants to organise themselves on a religious basis and when they favour the emergence of community spokesmen.

The West has often made this mistake in its dealings with the rest of the world. For centuries it was incapable of applying to other people – especially those whose destinies it controlled – the same principles it applied to its own, principles that were the source of its greatness. That is why France as a colonial power, for example, in order to avoid granting the inhabitants of its Algerian *départements* full citizenship, restricted them to the status of 'French Muslims', a rather anomalous designation in a secular republic.

It is important to remember the mistakes of the past in order to avoid repeating them. In colonial times, relations between the dominant and the dominated could not have been anything but unhealthy, since the genuine desire to 'civilise' the Other was constantly in conflict with the cynical desire to subjugate him. It must be acknowledged, as Hannah Arendt says in *The Origins of Totalitarianism*, that nation states make very poor empire-builders, since empire-building needs to be accompanied by a certain respect for the peoples you want to gather together. Alexander the Great dreamed of mass marriages between Hellenes and Persians; Rome cherished Athens and Alexandria and ended up granting Roman citizenship to all the subjects of its empire, from Celtic Druids to the Bedouins of Arabia. Closer to our own time, the Austro-Hungarian and Ottoman empires sought to be inclusive, with varying degrees of success. But the colonial empires built by European nations in the nineteenth and twentieth centuries were never more than extensions of themselves, schools of applied racism and moral transgression that prepared the way for the wars, genocides and totalitarianism that were to steep Europe in blood.

Our period offers the West the chance to restore its moral credibility, not by donning sackcloth and ashes, nor in opening itself up to all the world's woes, nor in compromising with values imported from elsewhere, but rather in showing itself at last to be true to its own values – respectful of democracy and human rights, concerned about equity, individual freedom and secularism – in its relations with the rest of the planet, and above all with the men and women who have chosen to live under its roof.

6

The attitude of Western countries towards their immigrants is not just one issue among many. In my view – and not just because I am an immigrant myself – it is a crucial question.

If the world is divided today between rival civilisations, it is principally in the minds of immigrants, both men and women, that a clash of civilisations occurs. It was no accident that the most bloody and spectacular terrorist attacks of recent years – in New York, Madrid, London and elsewhere – were carried out by immigrants, some from the Indian subcontinent, others from North Africa or Egypt, such as the Islamist militant who directed the attack on the Twin Towers of the World Trade Center and who had just completed his doctorate in urbanism at a German university. At the same time, many migrants take part peacefully and generously in the intellectual, artistic, social, economic and political life of their new countries, contributing new ideas, rare skills, different sounds, tastes and sensibilities, allowing those societies to be in tune with the world, giving them the ability to know it intimately in all its diversity and complexity.

So I say unambiguously, choosing my words with care: it is above all among immigrants that the great battle of our time, a battle for hearts and minds, will have to be waged, and it is among them that it will be won or lost. Either the West will manage to win them back, to regain their confidence, to rally them to the values it espouses, making them into eloquent advocates in its relations with the rest of the world. Or they will become its biggest problem.

The battle will be tough and the West is no longer in a very good position to win it. In the past, the only things hindering its room for manoeuvre were economic constraints and its own cultural prejudices. Today, it has a formidable adversary to deal with: all those people whose identities have been crushed for so long and whose thoughts have turned murderous. All that immigrants in the past, like colonial peoples, asked for was that the ruling power behave more like a mother than a stepmother. Their children, whether out of bitter disappointment, pride, weariness or impatience, no longer want that sort of relationship. They brandish the symbols of their origins and sometimes act as though their adoptive homes were enemy territory. The integration machine, which used to work, albeit rather slowly, has ground to a halt, sometimes as a result of deliberate sabotage.

For someone like me, who has lived in Europe for over thirty years and observed the coexistence of different ethnic communities slowly breaking down in numerous countries despite the fact that they practise quite different immigration policies, there is a strong temptation to throw up one's hands. I cannot be the only one to have had the depressing feeling that no approach brings the desired result — neither the strictest nor the most permissive; neither the ambitious republican model, which is supposed to make every immigrant to France entirely French, nor the pragmatic model from across the Channel, which accepts each community's uniqueness without trying to make it English.

Equally distressing, for the concerned observer such as myself, have been the murder of the Dutch film-maker Theo van Gogh, the demonstrations linked to the Danish cartoons, and dozens, hundreds of other worrying symptoms which have happened in almost every country and are replete with physical or moral violence.

It is just a short step from this to the conclusion that there is no point trying to integrate immigrants from the Muslim world or Africa. It is a step which many people have already taken silently, even if they still feel obliged to deny it. I, however, continue to believe that harmonious coexistence is possible and is in fact indispensable if we wish to forge solid links between the members of different cultures rather than resign ourselves to divisions between them which breed conflict, hatred and violence. Immigrants who fully embrace a sense of belonging to two cultures are more likely than anyone to break down divisions.

That said, I am conscious of the fact that successful integration today is arduous and will only become more so in the decades to come, and that thoughtful, subtle, patient and even resolutely willed action will be required to avoid looming disaster.

In France, generous spirits explain with varying degrees of conviction that successive waves of immigrants – Italians,

Poles, or refugees from the Spanish Civil War – have had to cope with hostility and prejudice before becoming fully integrated and that immigrants from the Muslim world will eventually follow a similar path. An admirable sentiment, but scarcely credible. The truth is that it will be hard for any European country to resolve its integration problems while the global atmosphere remains charged with mistrust and resentment, as it is today.

What happens in each country depends in part on the policies it implements, but it also depends in large measure on factors it cannot control. When someone from North Africa emigrates to the Netherlands, he arrives with an image of that country that has been conveyed by friends and family who have already gone there; but also with an image of the West as a whole, an image which is much more linked to US policy, or the memory of French colonialism, than the history of the Netherlands itself. This perception includes both positive aspects – otherwise he would not have come to live there – and negative ones, which today occupy a much bigger place than they did thirty years ago.

New immigrants observe the behaviour of their hosts with intense attention. They are constantly on the lookout for glances, gestures, words, whispers and silences that confirm that they are in a hostile or contemptuous environment. Of course, immigrants do not all react in the same way. Some are embittered and interpret everything that emanates from the Other negatively, while others are blissfully happy and only notice things which seem to show that they are accepted, valued or loved. Sometimes the same person will go from one feeling to another: a friendly smile makes him respond with overwhelming gratitude; an instant later, a word or gesture suggestive of hostility, contempt or simply a certain condescension and he feels a desire to lash out, break things and also to destroy himself. Because he hates his own image as much as the mirror which reflects it.

What makes relations fragile between immigrants and the societies which accept them – and as a result makes coexistence fragile too – is that the wound is always there. The skin that has formed on the surface has never been able to toughen. Anything at all can reawaken the pain, sometimes just a scratch or even a clumsy caress. In the West, many people shrug their shoulders at such hypersensitivity. Shouldn't we let bygones be bygones and forget colonialism, segregation, the treatment of the blacks, the extermination of the bushmen, the Taínos, or the Aztecs, the Opium Wars and the crusades? But the past does not occupy the same mental space for everyone, nor for every society.

7

For the past truly to become the past, it is not enough simply for time to go by. For a society to be able to draw a line between its past and its present, it needs something on this side of the hypothetical border on which to base its dignity, self-respect and identity. It needs among its attributes recent scientific inventions, convincing economic successes, cultural creations which are admired by others, or military victories.

Western nations do not have to look to distant centuries for reasons to be proud. Their contributions to medicine, mathematics or astronomy can be found in the morning papers. They do not need to invoke the contemporaries of Avicenna, or endlessly bring up the origins of terms such as 'zero', 'zenith', 'algebra' or 'algorithm'. Their most recent military victory dates from 2003, or 2001 or 1999; there is no need to go back to the ages of Saladin, Hannibal or Ashurbanipal. As a result, westerners do not feel the need to keep harking back to their past. If they do study it, it is to get a better view of their journey, to reveal trends, to under-stand, speculate or extrapolate. But this is not vital nor a requirement of their identity. The present is enough to confirm their self-esteem.

Conversely, people whose present offers only examples of failure, defeat, frustration and humiliation inevitably scour their past for reasons to keep believing in themselves. The Arabs feel like exiles in the contemporary world, strangers everywhere, scarcely less in their own countries than in the diaspora. They feel defeated, discredited and humiliated. They express it, shout it, lament it, and wonder constantly – explicitly or implicitly – how they might reverse the direction of history.

All oriental peoples in the past few centuries have felt the same. All of them have had to measure themselves against the West at some point; all have borne the brunt of its extraordinary energy, its formidable economic and military effectiveness, and its spirit of conquest. All have admired, feared, detested and fought it with different outcomes – the Chinese, Indians, Japanese, Iranians, Turks, Vietnamese, Afghans, Koreans and Indonesians, as well as the Arabs.

None of these peoples could recount their history without a thousand references to their encounter with the West, which sometimes lasted centuries. The whole modern history of a great country like China could be expressed around one central question: how to respond to the formidable challenge posed by the white man. All their major upheavals – whether the Boxer Rebellion, the rise of Mao, the 'Great Leap Forward', the Cultural Revolution or the new economic policy initiated by Deng Xiaoping – could in large measure be interpreted as the search for a response to that question. The question could also be reformulated like this: in order to be able to join the modern world without losing our dignity, what should we preserve of our past and what should we reject?

This is a question which never totally disappears from the consciousness of any human society, but it is not asked with the same intensity in all times and places.

When a nation achieves success, others look on it differently, which influences its self-image. I am thinking in particular of the attitude of the rest of the world to Japan and later China. Criticised, feared, but respected for their ability to fight, and in particular admired for their economic miracles, these countries have seen respect rise for everything their culture does: their languages, their art, their ancient and modern literature, their ancient medicine, their spiritual disciplines, their culinary traditions, their ritual dances, their martial arts and even their superstitions have attracted enthusiastic attention. As soon as a people acquires the image of being a winner, every aspect of its civilisation is looked at with interest and automatic respect by the rest of the world. The country itself may thereafter allow itself the luxury of becoming detached and critical. Indeed, the Chinese today often behave indifferently towards their past and feign amusement and incomprehension when Western visitors marvel at a civilisation dating back millennia.

*   *   *

Will the Arabs soon be in a similar position, thanks to the renaissance which began in 2011? Will they be able to regain the world's respect for themselves and also for their civilisation? One can hope, though it will take time to restore an image which has been deteriorating for decades, or indeed centuries. As they had suffered defeat after defeat, everything that constituted their civilisation was looked down on by the rest of the world. Their language was disparaged, their literature little read, their faith aroused mistrust, the spiritual masters they venerate were ridiculed. They themselves felt within their very souls the scorn of others and in the end they internalised and adopted it. The destructive feeling of self-hatred spread within many of them. I have written 'them' but I could have written 'us'; I feel myself an equal distance from both pronouns, just as near or far, and it may be that the additional tragedy of my people is reflected in this uncertainty.

There is no need to launch into 'wild' psychoanalysis to see that such as attitude gives rise to contradictory impulses: the desire to take it out on a cruel world and to do away with oneself; the desire to shed one's identity and yet assert it before the world; a loss of confidence in one's past, which one nonetheless clings on to because when one's identity has been scorned, it represents a lifeline, a refuge and a place of asylum.

What is true of the past is also true of religion. Islam is a place of refuge for identity as well as dignity. The conviction that one belongs to the true faith and has been promised a better world, while westerners have gone astray, lessens the shame and hurt of being a pariah, a loser, eternally defeated in this world. Indeed, it was until the uprisings of 2011, perhaps the only one in which Muslims still had a sense of being blessed among nations, of being chosen by the Creator rather than cursed and rejected.

As the lot of the Arabs progressively deteriorated on the ground, and as their armies were beaten and their lands occupied, and as their people were persecuted and humiliated and their enemies behaved arrogantly as though they were all-powerful, the religion which they have given the world became the last refuge of their self-respect. To abandon it would be to renounce their main contribution to universal history; in a sense, it would be to renounce the very purpose of their existence.

As a result, the question which arose and still arises in Muslim societies in this age of pain is not so much about the relationship between religion and politics as between religion and history, religion and identity, and religion and dignity. The way in which religion is lived in Islamic countries reflects the historical dead end in which these people found themselves trapped until recently, and from which they are only just beginning to emerge; if they succeed in freeing themselves from depotism, subjugation and humiliation, they will find verses which accord with democracy, modernity, secularism, coexistence, the primacy of knowledge and the glorification of life; their relation to the scriptures would become less nit-picking, less sensitive and less rigid. Forgive me repeating once again: the problem does not lie in the texts; nor does the solution.

★   ★   ★

There is no doubt that since the beginning of the twenty-first century the Muslim world's historical impasse has been one of the most obvious symptoms of the decline towards which a blindfold world seemed inevitably to be heading. Was it the fault of the Arabs, the Muslims, the way they live their religion? In part, yes. Is it not equally the fault of the West and the way it has for centuries managed its relations with other peoples? Yes, in part. And in the course of the past few decades, have the Americans and Israelis not borne a more specific responsibility? Probably. All these protagonists must radically change their behaviour if we are to see an end to a situation which starts from the open wound of the contemporary Middle East and is beginning to spread its gangrene to the whole planet, threatening to undermine all our civilisation's achievements.

That is a statement of the obvious which sounds like a pious wish, but it cannot be dismissed with a shrug. Is it already too late to put in place a historical compromise which at the same time takes into account the tragedy of the Jewish people and of the Palestinians, the Muslim world, the Eastern Christians, and also the impasse that the West has got into?

Even when if the horizon seems dark and the protagonists' demands seem irreconcilable, we must keep looking for traces of a solution.

One such, which could be promising, would be if the Jewish and Arab diasporas, instead of replicating the exhausting, sterile conflict which debilitates the Middle East, took the initiative to create a healthy rapprochement with the support of international diplomatic efforts.

Is it not much easier for an Arab and a Jew to meet and

talk calmly, to share a meal and socialise, if they live in Paris, Rome, Glasgow, Barcelona, Chicago, Stockholm, São Paulo or Sydney, rather than in Beirut, Algiers, Jerusalem or Alexandria? In the wide world where diasporas coexist, couldn't they sit down side by side, begin to forge links and reflect together on an alternative future for the people they hold dear in the Middle East?

That is happening already, one might reply. Perhaps, but much less than it ought to. On this crucial subject, I shall say what I have already said about several others: the question is not whether the Arabs and Jews talk to each other a bit more than they used to, or whether links are being made between people. The question is whether they will be able to resolve an endless conflict which is poisoning their lives and contributing to a disordered world.

8

The wish I have just expressed about the role of diasporas is linked to a wider hope that concerns all migrant populations, wherever they are, wherever they are from and whatever their history has been.

They all have powerful ties with two worlds at once, and they have authority to be communication channels, interfaces in both directions. If it is natural for a migrant to defend an attitude which comes from his home country in his new one, it should be just as natural for him to defend an attitude he acquired in his new country in his homeland.

It is sometimes said that if the Arab-Muslim immigrants of Europe formed a nation, it would be bigger than most member states of the EU, younger than all of them, and certainly the fastest-growing. What this overlooks is that if this population were an Eastern nation, it would not be negligible in terms of its size either, and it would be right at the top of the scale of all qualitative measures: its level of education, its spirit of enterprise, its experience of freedom, its active familiarity with the material and intellectual tools of modernity, its daily practice of coexistence, its ability to know widely varied cultures intimately, and so on. All of this

gives these migrants a potential influence possessed by no
other population in the East or the West.

It is an influence that they should exercise much more
than they do – with confidence, pride and in both directions
at once.

It is too readily forgotten that an immigrant is first of all an
emigrant. This is not just a banal shade of meaning; the
person really is double and lives as such. He belongs to two
different societies, with a different status in each. Take the
graduate who does a menial job in the city where he is an
exile, yet who in the village he comes from may be a person
of note. Or take the Moroccan worker who on the building
sites in the North speaks only timidly with his eyes lowered,
yet turns out to be a confident, voluble storyteller who
makes expansive gestures when he is with his own people
and is at last able to speak his language proudly. Or the
Kenyan nurse who spends her nights in a suburban hospital
and makes do with lukewarm soup and a piece of bread for
her meals, but is revered in her home province because each
month she sends back enough money to feed twelve family
members.

I could go on quoting examples indefinitely. What I am
trying to say is that we miss something essential when we fail
to see the emigrant behind the immigrant. And we commit
a major strategic error when we calculate the status of immigrants according to the place they occupy in Western
societies, which is often at the bottom of the social ladder,
rather than the role they play – and which they could play
much more effectively – in the societies they come from,

that of vectors of modernisation, social progress, intellectual liberation, development and reconciliation.

Because, I repeat, this influence can be exercised in both directions. You can live in Europe and endlessly dwell on the conflicts in Algeria, Bosnia or the Middle East, but equally you can convey to the Middle East, Bosnia or Algeria the European experience of the past sixty years: that of Franco-German reconciliation; the building of the Union; the fall of the Wall; the miraculous, definitive end to the era of dictatorship and colonial expeditions; the era of bloody butchery, massacres, genocide, centuries-old hatreds, leading towards an era of peace, harmony, freedom and prosperity.

What would have to happen for such a change in the way influence flows to come about? Migrants would have to want to transmit a constructive message to the societies they came from. That is easy to say, but difficult to put into practice, because it demands a radical change in our habits of mind and our behaviour.

So, for immigrants to want to become advocates for the European experience, they would have to fully identify with it; they would have to cease to be the targets of discrimination, humiliation, paternalism and condescension every time they show their 'typical' faces, utter their names or speak their language. They would have to identify spontaneously with their adoptive society and feel invited to immerse themselves in it body and soul.

But it is not enough for a migrant to identify with his adoptive country; in order for him to influence the society he comes from, it too has to continue to recognise him and recognise itself in him. Which entails that he will be able to assume his double identity with equanimity as fully as possible. Today that is not the case, neither in the French nor in the British approach to the question, to return to these two illustrative examples.

In France, the idea that governs the treatment of the immigrant question, as formerly with colonial peoples, is that every human being is capable of becoming French and must be helped to achieve it. A generous idea, born in the Enlightenment era, and one which would have changed the face of the world if it had been honestly applied in territories as diverse as Indochina, Algeria and Madagascar. It is an idea which more than ever remains respectable in its essence and even indispensable. From the moment when someone decides to live in a country other than the one he was born in, it is important that he is absolutely clear that he and his children will shortly be able to belong fully to the host nation. This aspect of the French approach consequently strikes me as having universal value; I certainly personally prefer this message to the British one, which tells the immigrant that he can keep his culture and customs, and that he will benefit from the protection of the law, but will remain an outsider in the nation which receives him.

In practice, however, neither of these approaches seems to me to suit our century; neither seems to me capable of assuring harmonious coexistence in the long term. Because in spite of their differences, these two policies start from the same supposition, namely that a person cannot belong fully to two cultures at once.

The immigrant in this new century needs to hear an entirely different message. He needs to be told in words and through attitudes and political decisions, 'You can become fully one of us without ceasing to be yourself.' That means, for example: 'You have the right and the duty to study our language in depth. But you also have the right and the duty not to forget your own language, because we, your adoptive nation, need people among us who share our values, understand our preoccupations and can speak Turkish perfectly, or Vietnamese, Russian, Arabic, Armenian, Swahili or Urdu, all the languages of Europe, Asia and Africa, every single one of them, so that we can make ourselves understood to all the people on the planet. You will be an invaluable intermediary between them and us in all domains – culture, politics and business.'

What an immigrant hungers for above all is dignity. And to be even more precise, cultural dignity. Religion is one element of this and it is legitimate for believers to want to practise their faith peacefully. But the most vital element of cultural identity is language. It is often because a language is neglected, including by an immigrant himself, and his culture discredited, including by himself, that an immigrant feels the need to show signs of his belief. Everything pushes him in this direction: the global atmosphere, the action of radical activists and also the behaviour of his new country where the authorities, obsessed with the immigrants' religious allegiances, fail to take account of their hunger for cultural recognition.

Sometimes it is even worse, since there is more mistrust towards linguistic pluralism, which is usually benign, than towards religious communitarianism, which for all pluralistic societies has constantly turned out to be a contributory factor to fanaticism, tyranny and disintegration.

I use the term 'communitarianism' deliberately. For me, it has a negative connotation, whereas 'pluralism' has a positive one. Because there is in fact a difference of kind between these two powerful identity factors, religion and language. Religious identity is exclusive; linguistic identity is not. Every human being is entitled to assemble within him- or herself several linguistic and cultural traditions.

I will not deny that my instinctive mistrust of religious communitarianism is linked in part to my origins. The Lebanon of my birth is probably the most emblematic example of a country dislocated by 'confessionalism', and as a result I feel no sympathy for this pernicious system. Perhaps it once was the answer to an ill, but in the long term it has turned out to be more harmful than the malady itself, like a drug that was administered to a patient to calm his suffering, but which created an irreversible addiction, which debilitated his body and mind a little more each day, to the point where it repaid him a hundredfold for all the pain it had temporarily spared him.

When I was young, I would have been more reticent about dwelling on this point, given that communitarianism seemed to be nothing more than a curious Levantine relic. Today, the phenomenon is global and sadly no longer looks like just a relic. The future of all humanity may well have its odious colouration.

For one of the most harmful consequences of globalisation is that it has globalised communitarianism. The rise in religious affiliations at the same time as the globalisation of communications encouraged the regrouping of people into 'global tribes' – an expression which, though it may seem like a contradiction in terms, is nonetheless a faithful reflection of reality. This is especially the case in the Muslim world, where there has been an unprecedented wave of communitarian particularism, which found its most bloody outlet in the conflict between Sunnis and Shi'ites in Iraq. But there has also been a sort of internationalism, which means an Algerian goes willingly to fight and die in Afghanistan, a Tunisian in Bosnia, an Egyptian in Pakistan, a Jordanian in Chechnya or an Indonesian in Somalia. This double movement of compartmentalisation and decompartmentalisation is not the least of the paradoxes of our times.

This is a worrying change, which it seems to me is explicable by the combined effect of major upheavals such as the failure of ideologies, which favoured the rise of assertions of identity and of those who advocated them; the computer revolution, which enabled solid and immediate links beyond all borders to be forged across seas, deserts and mountain ranges; and the rupture in the balance between power blocs, which posed a sharp question about power and its legitimacy at global level. In addition, the emergence of one dominant superpower, long seen as the champion of a single 'tribe', probably contributed to giving strategic rivalries a strongly identity-based association.

It is in the light of all of these factors that I can say, thinking in anguish of Lebanon, my homeland: ultimately, communitarianism was a dead end. Our fathers' generation should never have got swallowed up in it. Then I add in the same breath, this time thinking of France, my adoptive country, and of all of Europe, which is today the land of my last hopes: it is not in 'communitarianising' immigrants that you will facilitate their integration and escape the clashes which are looming, but by restoring social dignity, cultural dignity, linguistic dignity to each person, and by encouraging him to adopt his dual identity and his role as a link with equanimity.

9

More than once without dwelling on it I have criticised the notion of a clash of civilisations. Perhaps I should now pause a moment for a fairer, more balanced assessment.

What is problematic in this theory which has had so much media attention is not its clinical diagnosis. Its interpretative framework does allow greater understanding of events since the fall of the Berlin Wall. Since identity politics gained the upper hand over ideologies, human societies have often reacted to political events according to their religious affiliations: Russia has become openly Orthodox; the EU sees itself implicitly as a group of Christian nations; the same appeals to combat reverberate in all Muslim countries. Consequently, it is not unreasonable to describe the contemporary world with reference to spheres of civilisation which are in conflict.

In my view, where supporters of this theory go wrong is in departing from their observations of the present to construct a general theory of history. To explain to us, for example, that the current predominance of religious affiliations is the normal state of the human species, to which it has returned after a long detour through a series of

universalist utopias; or that the clash between civilisations is
the key which allows us to decipher the past and predict the
future.

Every theory of history is the child of its time. It is highly
instructive as a tool for understanding the present. When
applied to the past, it reveals itself to be approximate and
partial. Projected on to the future, it becomes risky and
sometimes destructive.

To see in today's conflicts a clash between six or seven
great civilisations – Western, Orthodox, Chinese, Muslim,
Indian, African, Latin-American – is enlightening and
intellectually stimulating, as is evidenced by the number of
debates it has given rise to. But this key does not help us
much to understand the great conflicts of human history:
think only of the First and Second World Wars, which
were principally quarrels among westerners and which
nonetheless shaped the world we all live in. And it does
not help us to explain monstrous phenomena which have
weighed on our contemporary moral consciousness, such
as totalitarianisms of the left as well as the right, or the
Holocaust; and that is not even to mention the great global
confrontation between capitalism and communism which
– from Spain to the Sudan, and China to Greece, Chile
and Indonesia – has profoundly divided societies belonging
to all civilisations.

More generally, when you look at various episodes of the
recent or distant past, you find in every period events such as
the crusades, which do indeed seem to reflect a clash of civilisations. But you also find that many others which are just as
significant and just as deadly occur within the Western

cultural sphere, or the Arab-Muslim, African or Chinese
one.

Even in our own era, which seems by and large to conform
to the academic schema of a clash of civilisations, an event
like the Iraq War clearly has several different facets: that of a
bloody conflict between the West and Islam; that of a yet
more bloody conflict within the Muslim world itself,
between Sunnis, Shi'ites and Kurds; and that of a clash
between great powers around the question of global
hegemony.

History, being composed of an infinity of individual events,
fits badly with generalisations. In order to find your way, you
need a large bunch of keys; and if it is legitimate for a
researcher to want to add the key he has forged himself, it is
unwise to want to replace the whole bunch with a single
key, a passkey which is supposed to open every door.

The twentieth century made abundant use of the key
offered by Marx and we now know what excesses that was
capable of leading to. Class struggle doesn't explain everything, and neither does the clash of civilisations. Not least
because the words themselves are ambiguous and deceptive. If everyone has a feeling of social belonging which
brings about class solidarity and also certain class hatreds,
the contours of this notion are fuzzy. At the time of the
industrial revolution, it was reasonable to think that the
emerging proletariat would become conscious of its identity, which would function as a distinct identity, as a 'class',
and play a determining role in history until the end of
time.

Could one say exactly the same of the new key provided by 'the clash of civilisations'. If everyone has a feeling of religious or ethnic belonging which brings about certain feelings of solidarity towards a civilisation, as well as the hatreds that go along with it, the contours of this notion are no less fuzzy than those of class. Today the zeitgeist leads us to believe that civilisations are defined entities, more and more conscious of their uniqueness, and that they will play a determining role in human history.

There is of course an element of truth here. Who could deny that Western civilisation is not to be confused with Chinese or Arab-Muslim civilisation? But no civilisation is watertight, none is immutable, and today the borders are more porous than in the past.

For millennia, our civilisations have been coming into being, developing, changing; they have come into contact and opposition with each other, imitated each other, differentiated themselves, allowed themselves to be copied; then, slowly or abruptly, they disappear or merge with others. Roman civilisation joined that of Greece one day. Each of them retained its character, but they also achieved an original synthesis which became a major element in European civilisation. Then Christianity came along, born in quite a different civilisation – principally Jewish, with Egyptian, Mesopotamian and more general Levantine influences – and became in turn an essential constituent of Western civilisation. Then the so-called barbarian peoples arrived from Asia – the Franks, Alamans, Huns, Vandals, Goths, all the Germanic peoples, the Altaics and the Slavs – who mixed with the Latins and Celts to form the nations of Europe.

Arab–Muslim civilisation was shaped in the same way. When the Arab tribes, including that of my ancestors, left their barren desert peninsula, their civilisation was schooled by Persia, India, Egypt, Rome and Constantinople. Then from the borders of China the Turkic tribes arrived, whose leaders remained our sultans and caliphs until after the birth of my own father, before being overthrown by a modernist nationalist movement which wanted to anchor its people firmly to European civilisation.

I say this by way of a reminder of the obvious fact that our civilisations have always been composite, shifting and permeable. And to express my surprise that today, when civilisations are more intermingled than ever, we are told that they are mutually implacable and destined to stay that way.

And what of today, now that thousands of Chinese party workers are trained in California and thousands of Californians dream of moving to China? Now that we have to make an effort as we travel the world to remember whether we have woken up in Chicago, Shanghai, Dubai, Bergen or Kuala Lumpur? Now that we are being told, on the strength of some examples of puzzling behaviour, that civilisations will remain distinct and that clashes between them will always be the driving force of history?

If our civilisations feel the need to affirm their uniqueness so stridently, it is precisely because their uniqueness is becoming indistinct.

What we are witnessing today is the twilight of distinct civilisations, not their advent or apotheosis. They have had their day and the time has come to transcend them all:

to capture their benefits and extend to the whole world the advantages of each, and to reduce their capacity for harm; to build a common civilisation little by little, based on two intangible and inseparable principles: the universality of essential values and the diversity of cultural expression.

To avoid any misunderstanding, let me add this: in my view, respecting a culture means encouraging the teaching of the language through which it is expressed, and promoting knowledge of its literature, theatre and cinema, and its other manifestations in art, architecture, craftsmanship, cuisine and so on. Conversely, being indulgent towards tyranny, oppression, intolerance or the caste system, or towards forced marriage, female genital mutilation, 'honour' crimes or the subjugation of women, towards incompetence, negligence, nepotism, widespread corruption, towards xenophobia or racism on the grounds that they emanate from a different culture, does not constitute respect in my view, but disguised contempt. It is the behaviour of apartheid, even if it is done with the best of intentions. I have said this already, but I am keen to repeat it in these final pages so that there is no ambiguity about what I believe cultural diversity is and is not.

I shall continue to use the broad term 'civilisation' in the singular and the plural. It seems perfectly legitimate to speak sometimes of human civilisations, and sometimes of human civilisation. Nations, ethnic groups, religions and empires all have their own particular courses. But the human race has its own adventure in which all of us, individuals and groups, are embarked.

It is only if we believe in this common adventure that we can make sense of our own specific journeys. And it is only if we believe that cultures possess equal dignity that we have the right to evaluate and even judge them, in accordance of course with values which are part of our common destiny and which are above all our civilisations, traditions and beliefs. For there is nothing more sacred than respect for human beings, the preservation of their physical and moral integrity, the preservation of their capacity to think and express themselves; and also the preservation of the planet on which they stand.

If we want this fascinating adventure to continue, we have to go beyond our tribal idea of civilisations and religions, free the former from the iron grip of ethnicity, rid the latter of the identity-based poison which distorts and corrupts them and turns them away from their spiritual and ethical vocation.

In this century, we shall have to choose between two visions of the future.

In the first, humanity is divided into global tribes which fight and detest one another but, as a result of globalisation, feed more every day on the same bland cultural broth.

In the second, humanity is aware of its common destiny and as a result is united around the same essential values, but continues to develop more than ever the richest, most diverse expressions of culture, preserving all its languages, artistic traditions, crafts, sensibility, memory, knowledge and so on.

On the one hand, then, we have several 'civilisations' which clash, but which imitate each other culturally and become homogeneous, and on the other a single human civilisation, but one which displays an infinite diversity.

To follow the first of these courses, all we need do is continue to drift along lazily, buffeted by shocks, as we do today. Choosing the second course will require a life-saving step change on our part. Are we up to it?

10

On this subject as on others, I am perpetually torn between extreme worry and hope. At times, I tell myself that in its darkest hours humanity always knows how to find the resources necessary to extricate itself, even at the cost of very heavy sacrifices. And at others, I tell myself it would be irresponsible always to expect a miracle.

My belief at the moment is that the paths to a solution are undeniably diminishing but that they are not yet closed off. What needs to be promoted is not despair but urgency. That is indeed the sole reason for this book's existence, from its first page to its last. To say that it is late, but not too late. To point out that it would be suicidal and criminal not to mobilise all our energies to prevent collapse and decline. To suggest that we can still take action, but that we must be bold and imaginative rather than weak-willed, timorous and conventional; that we must dare to overturn our usual thought patterns and ways of behaving, upset our imaginary certainties and rebuild our scale of priorities.

Of all the threats awaiting us in this century, the most perceptible today, as well as the best-studied and documented, is climate change. There is every reason to believe that in the decades ahead it will provoke cataclysmic disturbances whose extent we are not yet able to measure. Sea levels may rise by several metres, engulfing many coastal cities and other maritime zones inhabited by hundreds of millions of people. Because of the disappearance of glaciers and changes to rainfall patterns, major rivers could dry up, condemning entire countries to desertification. One can imagine the tragedies – massive displacements of people, deadly struggles – which could result from such a trend.

This development does not belong to a vague and distant future. We already know that it will dramatically affect the existence of our children and grandchildren; it is probable that the generations born in the second half of the twentieth century will still have time, I dare say, to suffer from it themselves.

I am a sceptic by temperament. When I hear alarm bells, I bridle, take myself to one side, and try to ascertain calmly whether we are being manipulated. We have often been told that apocalyptic disasters are coming, only to find a few months or even weeks later that they have vanished, thank God, leaving no trace. Will it not be just the same with climate change? Were we not told just a few decades ago that the world was in fact heading for a new ice age? Writers and film-makers seized upon this theme with varying degrees of success.

So when I started hearing warnings about a global warming rather than cooling, the news naturally aroused my curiosity without greatly diminishing my scepticism.

★   ★   ★

When scientific studies became more numerous and insistent and when their results began to agree, I wanted to learn more.

Lacking a scientific education worthy of the name, I had first to plunge into the most elementary books in order to understand what was being said and to understand the much-discussed 'greenhouse effect', how it works and why it has been causing so much concern for some time. To understand what the increase in CO_2 in the atmosphere means, and what its causes and consequences could be. To understand also why there is such fear about the Greenland and Antarctic ice sheets melting, but less about the melting of the Arctic Ocean, which it is now possible to cross in a boat from one side to the other during the summer months for the first time in millennia.

Am I going to say that at the end of my investigation I can verify that this phenomenon is serious and that it constitutes a threat to human civilisation? That is indeed the deep conviction I came to; but – and I say this in all sincerity – my judgement in this matter does not count for very much. In matters of science, the opinion of a layperson such as me does not merit being taken into consideration. To use a term which keeps coming up in my analysis, I have no intellectual legitimacy in this field. However, as a man who cares about the well-being of those who are dear to him, as a responsible citizen, worried by the excesses of the human adventure, and as a writer who is attentive to the debates which animate his contemporaries, I cannot shrug and make do with the conclusion that only the future will tell us whether we have been too alarmist or too disbelieving, too pusillanimous, and that we will find out in thirty years who was right and who was wrong.

Waiting for the judgement of the future means running a terrible risk. If it is true that in thirty years the damage caused by climate change has become irreparable, and if it is true that planet earth will already have gone out of control, that it will function erratically and ultimately uncontrollably, it would be absurd, suicidal and even criminal to wait for the future's verdict.

So what should we do? Act before we are certain that the threat is real? Act even if we were to discover in thirty years that the Cassandras were wrong? My answer – though I admit it is paradoxical – is yes, we must act, and even if we have remaining doubts, we must behave as if we do not.

This attitude may seem irrational. But for once I would own up to it without a hint of hesitation. Not based on my deep conviction, which, though informed, concerns no one but myself. Nor simply because an overwhelming majority of scientists are convinced of the reality of global warming, and that its causes are linked to human activity, and also that this change poses a deadly threat to the future of the planet and its inhabitants. This near-unanimous consensus cannot be disregarded and I of course take it into account, but it does not constitute the last word in my view. The majority is not always right, and scientists have been wrong before. However, I believe that we ought to heed them in matters of climate change and as a consequence we must act, even before we are certain they are right.

To clarify my position, I shall formulate a wager, inspired by the one devised in the past and in a quite different context by

the incomparable Blaise Pascal. With, however, a difference
of scale: the result of Pascal's wager could only be checked in
the afterlife, whereas it will be possible to check our wager
here on earth relatively soon, since the vast majority of those
who currently inhabit our planet will still be alive.

I shall therefore consider the two principal reactions to
climate change – the inadequate and then the adequate one
– and try to imagine the consequences each of them would
entail.

The first hypothesis is that no major step change occurs.
Some countries make efforts to limit their greenhouse gas
emissions; others react more half-heartedly with no more
than cosmetic measures, so as to avoid appearing to be
bottom of the class. Still others do nothing at all, for fear of
harming their economic activity or upsetting their consumption patterns, and therefore continue to pollute quite happily.
As a result, the concentration of carbon dioxide in earth's
atmosphere keeps rising.

On this reckoning, where will the world be in thirty
years? If we believe the majority of scientists, as well as the
United Nations and all the international organisations
which keep sounding the alarm, we will be on the brink of
apocalypse, because we will have passed the point at which
we can prevent our planet from running totally out of
control. Without going into too much detail, I shall limit
myself to signalling two pieces of evaluation data which
strike me as particularly worrying.

The first is that the rise in the planet's temperature, which
is a consequence of the greenhouse effect, will cause the
evaporation of water from the oceans, which in turn will

increase the greenhouse effect. In other words, we could
enter a vicious circle of warming which will no longer be
dependent on anthropogenic greenhouse gas emissions, but
will accelerate by itself and become virtually impossible to
stop. When do we risk reaching this tipping point? Opinions
vary, but some think that it could kick in as early as the first
quarter of this century. What is certain is that the longer we
take to react, the more painful and costly the efforts we shall
have to make.

The second piece of data, which points in the same direction, is that dramatic climate events may happen very
suddenly, much more so than is currently thought. By way
of example, it is thought today that the last swing from a
glacial to a temperate period, which took place around
11,500 years ago, happened not by a slow process over centuries or millennia, but suddenly, in no more than a decade.
Moreover, numerous scientists who have been studying
climate-related phenomena for decades have been constantly
surprised by the rapidity of changes, which often go far
beyond the forecasts of what was thought plausible. All of
which means that we must not imagine that everything we
are talking about will not have consequences before the end
of this century or into the following ones. We really cannot
tell, and it would be wise to start preparing immediately for
the worst-case scenario.

In thirty years – I am sticking to this figure so as to remain
within the framework of a period which is meaningful in
terms of a human lifespan, and which allows my generation
still to speak of 'us' – we may not have witnessed all the
changes which loom on the horizon, but we will already

have had some devastating examples. And more seriously, the whole of humanity will have to endure a state of emergency for decades and the imposition of heavy sacrifices which will be difficult to bear without even the assurance that we can still prevent our descent into the abyss.

What if the majority were wrong? What if the future vindicated the dissenting minority which rejects the cataclysmic forecasts, mocks their alarmism and questions any link between our gas emissions and global warming; and which sometimes does not even believe in the reality of global warming, reckoning rather that we are witnessing natural temperature cycles which oscillate down then up, then down again, for all sorts of reasons which depend much more on the sun's activity than humans'?

Once again, I am not qualified to refute these arguments and I want to suppose here that they could turn out to be true. If that is the case, we could not but rejoice. Many people would have to eat their hats with whatever grace they can muster: scientists, political leaders, international officials and everyone who believed them and relayed their fears – including me, if I am still around.

And now for the second hypothesis: humanity takes action. Benefiting from the political changes in the US, we see a major step change. Draconian measures are taken to reduce significantly fossil fuel consumption and carbon concentrations in the atmosphere. The rate of global warming slows, sea levels do not rise and no major drama linked to climate change takes place.

At this prospect, I imagine a debate between two scientists thirty years from now. One belongs to the majority consensus and supports the view that it was thanks to this step change that humanity escaped a global catastrophe which would have threatened its survival. The other belongs to the dissenting minority and continues stubbornly to insist that the dangers were grossly exaggerated and even simply an illusion. It is unlikely there would be agreement between them. Since the 'patient' is still alive, how can it be conclusively shown that he was in mortal danger? The two doctors by his bedside could debate indefinitely.

However, at one point in their discussion, the first scientist might say to the other: 'Let's forget our past quarrels and simply ask ourselves: isn't our planet much healthier as a result of the course of treatment it followed? I will continue to maintain that it was in mortal danger and you will continue to doubt it, but weren't our countries right to reduce their consumption of fossil fuels and their pollution from factories and power stations?'

And that is the basis of the wager I have formulated about climate change: if we proved incapable of altering our behaviour and the threat turned out to be real, we would have lost everything. If we did manage to change our behaviour radically, and the threat turned out to be illusory, we would not have lost anything at all. Because the measures which would allow us to face the threat of climate change are in reality, when you think about it, measures which are worth taking in any case – in order to reduce pollution and its harmful effects for public health; in order to reduce the threat of poverty and social upheavals which climate change could provoke; in order to avoid savage conflicts for control of oil fields, mining regions and water supplies; and in order for humanity to progress in greater serenity.

Consequently, it is not up to the majority of scientists to show that the threat is real. It is, rather, up to the dissenting minority to show irrefutably that the danger is completely illusory. The burden of proof is reversed, as a lawyer might put it. It is only if we are absolutely sure that this mortal danger does *not* exist that we would have the moral right to drop our guard and continue on our way without changing any of our habits.

Of course, such certainty is out of the question. The stakes are so high that no one – no researcher, industrialist, economist, political leader, intellectual, no sensible being – could take the responsibility for asserting, against the view of the vast majority of scientists, that risks linked to climate change do not exist and that we should simply ignore them.

In this field more than the others, all we can do is anxiously wonder which path humanity will take – that of a step change or that of business as usual.

The times we are living in give contradictory signs. On the one hand, our awareness is real and the weight of the US, which too long pushed down on the wrong side of the scales, should now tip the balance in the opposite direction. However, the hoped-for step change requires a level of solidarity and even a profound bond between nations which is not easy to achieve. And it demands sacrifices.

Are the countries of the North prepared to disrupt their way of life? Are emerging nations, especially China and

India, ready to put at risk their economic take-off, the first chance they have had in centuries to escape underdevelopment? That supposes at the very least vast concerted global action, from which everyone gets something and no one feels hard done by.

I want to believe that such an effort is possible, but I cannot easily overcome my worries when I look at our world: a world characterised by profound asymmetry in international relations; a world in the grip of identity-based tribalism and supreme selfishness, in which moral credibility remains a rare commodity; a world in which great crises generally push nations, social groups, companies and individuals to protect their own interests fiercely rather than demonstrate solidarity or generosity.

AFTERWORD

I

What we see unfolding at the start of this century is no ordinary kind of turbulence. For the globalised world born out
of the ruins of the Cold War, it may be that this turbulence
will shake us out of a too lengthy prehistory both morally
and intellectually, and help found a new world. But equally,
it may turn out to cause destruction and disintegration and
be the prelude to painful decline.

Will a way be found for the world's populations – which
evolution has forced into permanent contact with each other
despite all their differences of religion, colour, language,
history and traditions – to coexist in peace and harmony?
The question is a real one in every country and every city, as
well as on a global level. And at present, the reply remains
uncertain. Whether we think of countries where different
communities have coexisted for centuries, or those which
have accepted significant numbers of immigrants within
recent decades, it is clear that mistrust and incomprehension
are growing to the point where all integration policies are
compromised, as is simple coexistence. Many elections and
debates today are weighed down by this thorny issue, which
encourages identity tensions and xenophobia, especially in

Europe, where some of the most tolerant societies have become irritated, embittered and entrenched over it. But at the same time, we have seen surprising reversals in the perception of the Other, stemming from less visible developments in people's attitudes, the most revealing and spectacular example being the advent of Barack Obama.

The global debate on coexistence is not going to go away. Violent or muted, explicit or implicit, it will remain with us throughout this century and for centuries to come. Our planet is a closely woven web of different populations, all of which are conscious of their identity and of the regard in which they are held by others; they are also aware of the rights they want to win or hold on to, and believe that they both need others and need to protect themselves from them. There is no point in waiting for the tensions between them to lose their edge simply with the passage of time. There are, after all, peoples who have lived side by side for centuries without ever achieving mutual respect or peaceful coexistence. Overcoming prejudices and hatred is not innate to human nature. Acceptance of others is no more or less natural than rejection. Reconciliation, uniting, adopting, taming and pacifying are acts of will, acts of civilisation which demand lucidity and perseverance; acts which need to be acquired, taught and cultivated. Teaching people to live together is a long struggle which is never completely won. It requires calm reflection, skilful teaching, appropriate legislation and effective institutions. Living in the Levant before emigrating to Europe, I often had occasion to observe the difference it made to a society when such a battle was fought with determination and subtlety as opposed to being neglected, or clumsily and incoherently executed.

Today that battle needs to be waged on a global scale for the whole of humanity, and also within each population. Clearly that is not yet happening, at least not enough. We talk constantly of the global village, and it is true that thanks to progress in communications, our planet has become a single economic space, as well as a single political and media space. But that makes mutual hatreds all the more apparent.

In particular, the rift between the West and the Arab-Muslim world has continued to grow in recent years, to the point where it now seems almost beyond repair. I am one of those who feel sorrow at this every day, but there are many who have got used to it and some who even relish it, ignoring the huge potential for violence that this clash may harbour, which casts a dark shadow over our common future. The deadly terrorist attacks which have blighted the past few years are examples of this potential. Those of 11 September 2001 have already entered our new century's history as a monstrous atrocity. Acts similarly inspired have taken place on every continent, from Nairobi to Madrid, Bali to London, via Djerba, Algiers, Casablanca, Beirut, Amman, Taba, Jerusalem, Istanbul, Beslan or Mumbai, not to mention Baghdad.

It is true that such attacks, however violent they may be, do not threaten to annihilate the world as the Soviet and American thermonuclear arsenals did during the Cold War. They could nonetheless turn out to be extremely deadly, especially if in the future they involve so-called

non-conventional weapons – chemical, biological, atomic or
something else. Moreover the resultant social, political and
economic   disruption   they   could   cause   would   be
devastating.

But I prefer to think that another major attack can be
avoided, which fortunately remains plausible. In the countries under the greatest threat, the authorities have reacted
firmly and effectively. So as not to be caught out, they are
trying to anticipate and detect the smallest risk. It would be
irresponsible to reproach them for this. However, it goes
without saying that a society which feels the need to protect
itself permanently from unscrupulous enemies inevitably
moves away from strict respect for laws and principles. As a
result, an enduring terrorist threat cannot but disrupt the
functioning of democracy in the long term.

One day we will remember these cursed years as those
when the most civilised police force in the world pinned a
young Brazilian commuter to the floor in the London
Underground; he was entirely innocent but his skin was
somewhat swarthy. He was summarily killed with seven
bullets to the head.

The clash of civilisations is not a debate about the respective
merits of Erasmus versus Avicenna, alcohol or the veil, or
over sacred texts. It is a global drift towards xenophobia,
discrimination, ethnic humiliation, massacres and reprisals.
In other words, the erosion of all that gives human civilisation its moral dignity.

In such an atmosphere, even those who are persuaded to
fight barbarism eventually succumb to it in their turn.

Terrorist violence begets anti-terrorist violence, which feeds resentment, facilitating the task of those who recruit extremists and paving the way for future attacks. Is a given population regarded with suspicion because it plants bombs, or does it plant bombs because it is regarded with suspicion? It is the old story of the chicken and the egg, and there is no point in seeking an answer, for there is none. Everyone will have their own answer, dictated by their fears, prejudices, origins and suffering. The vicious circle needs to be broken, but from the moment the mechanism is set in motion, it is hard to withdraw your hand.

How can one not fear decline in such a context? If the current hostility between the planet's various tribes were to persist, and the disorder in all fields go on, the world would experience an erosion of democracy, the rule of law and all social norms in the course of this century.

I for one refuse to consider this inevitable, but it is clear that we shall have to deploy the full range of our ingenuity, vision and determination to stand any chance of avoiding it.

2

Since I began work on this book, an allegorical image has haunted me: a group of climbers is scaling a cliff and, because of some sudden shock, they have begun to lose their footing. I have been trying to understand why these men risk coming unstuck and how they could reattach themselves to the rock face in order to resume their ascent, without dwelling too much on imagining what would happen if they fell into the abyss.

I speak of it in terms of a mountaineering accident, as that is rather how it seems when I reflect on the course of the world. I am not unaware that, in history, the notion of an accident is often deceptive. However, I am not going to abandon it entirely. Whatever contemporary and past moralists have said, humanity does not deserve the punishment that the coming decades might inflict. Nor shall I plead innocence, or put it down to bad luck or the quirks of fate. However, I believe that what is happening to us, rather than being the consequence of our failures and oversights, is in fact the consequence of our successes, our accomplishments, our legitimate ambitions, our equally legitimate freedom and the incomparable genius of our species.

In spite of the things that irritate and worry me, I remain fascinated by the human adventure; I cherish and venerate it and nothing in the world would persuade me to exchange it for the life of an angel or a beast. We are Prometheus's children; Creation has been entrusted to us and we must continue it. We have undertaken the task of reshaping the universe and if there is a supreme Creator above, we merit His pride as much as His wrath.

Are we not now paying the price for this Promethean boldness and the frantic race to the summit? Probably, but we have no reason to be repentant – not for our inventions, even the craziest, nor for the freedoms we have won. And if the moment has come to wonder much more seriously than in the past and with greater urgency, 'Where are we rushing to?', the question should be asked not in a spirit of contrition or denigration, nor with an implication that we are going too fast, departing from the path or losing our bearings, but as a genuine question.

This century resounds with the most backward-looking rhetoric. It could mark the moment of revenge for all those who have always hated man's liberation and even more so that of woman; for those who distrust science, art, literature and philosophy; for those who would like to return the mass of humanity like docile sheep to the reassuring fold of age-old moral tyrannies. But if we have strayed from the path, it is not from the path our fathers beat, but from the one we should be beating for our children, a path which no generation before us has had the chance to glimpse and which no other has so vitally needed.

I want to underline this here as I did in the book's opening pages, because reactions to the turbulence of our times may take very different forms. I shall distinguish three, which, to remain with the mountaineering metaphor, I shall call the temptations of the precipice, the rock face and the summit.

The 'temptation of the precipice' is characteristic of our age. Every day, men leap into the void hoping to take the whole climbing party with them. This is a phenomenon without any real precedent in history. These people, however numerous they may be, represent only the burning fuse of a giant powder keg of despair. Hundreds of millions of their fellow human beings in the Muslim world and elsewhere feel the same temptation, which the overwhelming majority fortunately resist.

It is not so much the sting of poverty which causes their distress as that of humiliation and insignificance, the feeling of not belonging in the world they live in, of being only losers, downtrodden and excluded. And so they dream of ruining the feast to which they have not been invited.

The 'temptation of the rock face' is much less characteristic of our age, but it has taken on a new meaning. What I have in mind here is the attitude which consists of bracing oneself, taking shelter and protecting oneself while waiting for the storm to pass. In other circumstances it would be the wisest option. But the tragedy for our and future generations is that this storm is not going to pass. The wind of history will continue to blow more and more strongly, and at ever greater speed, and nothing and no one will be able to calm or slow it.

I shall not speak of those who hold this attitude as a section of humanity, since the temptation exists in all of us. It is hard for us to accept that the world has to be entirely reconceived, that the road to the future needs to be sketched by our own hands, that our ordinary, peaceful, insignificant behaviour could trigger a major climate disaster and turn out to be just as suicidal as hurling ourselves into the void. And it is hard to accept that our age-old attachments based on identity could compromise the advance of the human species. And so we try to persuade ourselves that there is nothing fundamentally new under the sun and continue to cling to our familiar footholds, our inherited allegiances, recurrent quarrels and flimsy certainties.

The 'temptation of the summit' is based on the opposite idea, namely that humanity has reached a dramatically new phase of its evolution in which the old formulas no longer work. It is not the end of history, as was prematurely declared when Communism fell, but it is probably the twilight of a certain *type* of history and also – I dare to believe and hope – the dawn of another.

What has had its day and now must end is the tribal phase of human history, the history of struggles between nations, states, ethnic and religious communities and civilisations. What we are witnessing coming to an end is the prehistory of mankind. It has been too long a prehistory, made up of all our identity-based tensions, all our blinding ethnocentricity, and a selfishness which is held to be sacred, whether based on country, community, culture, ideology or something else.

It is not my intention here to pass ethical judgement on

the time-worn mechanisms of history as we know it, but to note that new realities mean we must leave them behind as soon as possible in order to embark on a completely new phase of the human adventure, a phase in which we shall not fight against the Other – the enemy nation, civilisation, religion or community – but against much more considerable, redoubtable enemies that threaten the whole of humanity.

When we set aside the debilitating habits we have acquired during our prehistory, it is abundantly clear that the only battles truly worth fighting for our species in the centuries ahead are scientific and ethical. Overcoming all illness; slowing the ageing process; making natural death retreat by several decades and perhaps one day by several centuries; freeing people from need as well as ignorance; giving them through art, knowledge and culture the inner richness which might furnish their ever-longer lives; conquering the vast universe, and all the while not damaging the ground on which we stand – those are the only conquests which should mobilise the energies of our children and theirs. I for one find those much more inspiring than any patriotic war, and as mentally stimulating as any mystical experience. It is towards such ambitions that we should now turn.

A pious wish, you may say. No, a necessity for survival and consequently the only realistic option. Having reached this advanced stage of its evolution, characterised by such a high degree of global integration, the only options for humanity are to collapse or change.

3

The phase of evolution I have just referred to is not an abstract concept. Never has humanity had such a need for effective solidarity and collective action to face the many dangers which assail it. They are huge dangers born of advances in science, technology and demographics, as well as the economy, and they threaten to destroy within a century everything that has been built over millennia. I am thinking of the proliferation of atomic weapons and other instruments of death. I am thinking of the exhaustion of natural resources and the return of great pandemics. Nor am I forgetting climate change, of course, which is perhaps the gravest danger humanity has had to face since the birth of the earliest civilisations.

But all these threats could also constitute an opportunity, if they allow us finally to open our eyes, to understand the scale of the challenges we have to face and the mortal risk we run if we do not change our behaviour, and do not rise – mentally and especially morally – to the level which our current stage of evolution demands.

I would be lying if I said that I have complete faith in our collective survival instinct. If such an instinct exists in individuals, it remains hypothetical for the species as a whole. At any rate, as a result of the various crises affecting us directly, it is now time to make up our minds. Either this century will be the one in which humanity goes into decline, or else it will be the century of a step change and beneficial transformation. If we needed a state of emergency to shake us up and mobilise what is best in us, we've got one.

I remain in a state of worried anticipation, but I also see some good reasons for hope. They are not all of the same sort and they do not all respond to the same levers, but, taken as a whole, they make it possible to imagine a different future.

The first reason for hope is that, in spite of the tensions, crises, conflicts and shocks, scientific progress continues at an increasing pace. It may seem out of place to mention among the positive signs today a tendency which has been going on for several generations. If I mention it nonetheless it is because the consistency of science may help us overcome the turbulence of this century. I shall not go so far as to say that scientific progress is the antidote to decline, but it is certainly one of its ingredients – on condition that we use it wisely, of course.

We can reasonably imagine, for example, that scientists will give us a whole range of clean technologies in the decades ahead, which will enable us to limit carbon emissions in the atmosphere so that we can escape the vicious circle of global warming. We must not imagine, however, that we can simply hand this problem over to them and continue in our current ways with a clear conscience. Our scientists probably do not have enough time to enable us to avoid the climate disturbances which could affect the planet in the first half of this century. We shall have to navigate round that difficult cape with the equipment we have on board; only afterwards will science be able to offer us long-term solutions.

My confidence in science is simultaneously limitless and cautious. To questions which are within its purview, I think it is capable in time of bringing complete answers and thereby giving us the means to realise our wildest dreams. This is simultaneously exciting and frightening, because man's dreams contain everything, both the best and the worst, and we cannot count on science to distinguish between them. Science is morally neutral, at the service of human wisdom and human folly. In the future, just as in the past and the present, it runs the risk of being led astray, turned to the profit of tyranny, greed or archaism.

My second reason for hope is not free from worries either. I have already spoken of it: it is the fact that the most populous nations on the planet are resolutely on the way to emerging from poverty. It is possible that in the years ahead we shall witness a slowing of this process, serious disturbances and even armed conflict. Nonetheless, we now know that underdevelopment is not a given and that the eradication of centuries-old blights such as poverty, hunger, endemic diseases and illiteracy cannot be considered a naive dream. What has been shown to be possible for three or four billion people ought to be possible for six, seven or eight billion in a few decades.

From the viewpoint of human solidarity, open to the future, this clearly is a major milestone.

★   ★   ★

My third reason for hope has its source in the experience of contemporary Europe. It symbolises to me an outline of what the end of prehistory could mean in concrete terms: gradually putting behind us accumulated hatreds, territorial quarrels and ancient rivalries; allowing the sons and daughters of those who killed each other to join hands and conceive the future together; organising a shared life for six nations, then nine, twelve or fifteen, then thirty; transcending the diversity of cultures without ever seeking to eradicate them; all of this so that one day one ethical homeland will be created out of many.

Throughout history, every time someone has spoken up to say that the different nations of the planet should be reconciled, draw closer to each other, jointly manage their shared living space and think of their common future, they have been called naive for preaching utopianism. The European Union, in fact, offers us the example of a utopia in the process of being created. As such it constitutes a pioneering experiment, a plausible foretaste of what humanity, having achieved reconciliation, may be in the future and proof that the most ambitious visions are not necessarily naive.

That said, the European endeavour is not without its flaws. Everyone involved in it sometimes expresses doubts. I feel some impatience with it myself. I would like Europe to set an example of coexistence among both its founding peoples and the immigrants it has taken in. I wish it would focus much more on its cultural dimension and manage its linguistic diversity much better. I wish it would resist much more strongly the temptation to be a club of rich white Christian nations and dare to see itself as a model for the rest of humanity. And on an institutional level I would like it to dare to build a single democratic unit, the European equivalent of the United States of America, in which states are endowed with a greater cultural specificity and take pains to defend and promote them, but with federal leaders whose authority is universally recognised, elected on the same day throughout the whole continent. I am also worried about examples of timidity I see and a certain moral short-sightedness.

But these reservations do not in any way diminish my faith in the exemplary value of the 'laboratory' that the creation of Europe represents for humanity at this crucial stage.

A fourth reason for hope occurred in the New World at the start of the amazing year of 2008: the rise of Barack Obama, as a symbol and as a man; the return of a forgotten America, that of Abraham Lincoln, Thomas Jefferson and Benjamin Franklin; in other words, the sudden reawakening of a great nation as a result of its economic crisis and military entanglements.

In response to the only other crisis of similar scale, which began in 1929, Franklin D. Roosevelt launched the New Deal, and it is indeed a new deal which the United States and the whole world need today. But it will have to be broader still and much more ambitious than that of the 1930s. This time it is not just a matter of relaunching the economy and restoring the importance of certain social questions. It is a matter of rebuilding a new global reality, new relations between nations and a new way of working for the planet which will put an end to the disorder in strategy, finance, ethics and climate; and in order for a superpower to commit itself to such a task, it must first recover the legitimacy of its global role.

I have said before that a people recognises itself in leaders who espouse its struggles. I would say the same thing applies at global level. For the world's nations to accept the primacy of one of their number, they have to be persuaded that that legitimacy is being exercised to their advantage and not at their expense.

Of course, the United States will always have enemies, rivals and even implacable foes who will fight it with all the greater determination if they see the rest of the world rally willingly around it. But the majority of people and leaders in Europe, Africa, Asia and Latin America will judge it on its actions. If it acts on the international stage with subtlety and fairness, if it forces itself to consult other nations respectfully rather than handing down diktats, if it makes it a point of honour to apply to itself first what it demands of others, if it clearly distances itself from immoral practices which have too often sullied its record throughout the world, and if it leads the global mobilisation against the economic crisis, global warming, epidemics, endemic disease, poverty, injustice and discrimination, then its role as first power will be accepted and applauded. Even the use of its military power will not provoke the same reactions of rejection, as long as it does not become a reflex action but remains exceptional and abides by recognisable principles, and is not accompanied with a string of bloody blunders.

More than ever, the world needs America, but an America which is reconciled with the world as well as with itself, an

America which exercises its global role with respect for its own values as well as others' – with integrity, fairness and generosity. I would even add with elegance and grace.

We shall have to wait many years for an adequate evaluation of the true impact of Barack Hussein Obama on the United States and the rest of the world. However, it seems to me that his presence in the White House is not unconnected with the dramatic changes which began in the Arab world in 2011. The fact that these huge protests have, for the first time in decades, been devoid of the least hostility to the United States is due at least in part to the fact that the young president, his personality, African origins, middle name and his subtle choice of the words he uses and avoids using, made the traditional anti-American rhetoric that usually resounds in Arab streets irrelevant and even anachronistic. And it may be that it was the disappearance of this outdated alibi which led the people to attack their own governments, whom they now saw as being truly responsible for their debasement and the first obstacles to demolish on the path to renewal.

I have mentioned some factors that enable us to keep hope alive. But the task to be accomplished is huge and cannot be entrusted to a single leader, however clear-sighted and persuasive he may be, nor to a single nation, however powerful, nor to a single continent.

Because it is not simply a matter of putting in place a new economic and financial model, a new system of international relations, nor only a matter of correcting some obvious types of disorder. It is rather an urgent matter of conceiving an entirely new vision of politics, the economy, work, consumption, science, technology, progress, identity, culture, religion and history, and implanting it in people's minds; it needs to be an adult vision of what we are, what others are, and the fate of the planet which we all share. In a nutshell, we need to 'invent' a conception of the world which is not just the modern version of our ancestral prejudices and which will allow us to ward off the decline that is on the horizon.

All of us who are living through these strange early years of the twenty-first century have the duty – and, more than any preceding generation, the means – to contribute to this rescue effort; with wisdom and lucidity, but also with passion and sometimes even with anger.

Yes, with the burning anger of the righteous.

Bibliography

Adams, Henry, *The Education of Henry Adams*, Oxford Paperbacks, 2008

Adler, Alexandre, *J'ai vu finir le monde ancien*, Grasset & Fasquelle, 2002

Albiac, Gabriel, *La Synagogue vide*, Presses Universitaires de France, 1994

Ansary, Tamim, *West of Kabul, East of New York*, Picador, 2003

Arendt, Hannah, *The Origins of Totalitarianism*, André Deutsch, 1986

Armstrong, Karen, *The Bible: A Biography*, Atlantic, 2007

Barnavi, Élie, *Les Religions meurtrières*, Flammarion, 2006

Bellati Ceccoli, Guido, *L'islam social*, Les Trois Anneaux, 2006

Boyle, T. C., *The Tortilla Curtain*, Bloomsbury, 1996

Bragg, Melvyn, *The Adventure of English: The Biography of a Language*, Hodder & Stoughton, 2003

Campbell, Greg, *Blood Diamonds: Tracing the Path of the World's Most Precious Stones*, Westview Press (US), 2004

Chandrasekaran, Rajiv, *Imperial Life in the Emerald City: Inside Baghdad's Green Zone*, Bloomsbury, 2007

Chomsky, Noam, *Hegemony or Survival: America's Quest for Global Dominance*, Hamish Hamilton, 2003

Clarke, Richard A., *Against All Enemies: Inside America's War on Terror*, The Free Press, 2004

Corm, Georges, *La question religieuse au XXIe siècle*, La Découverte, 2006

Courbage, Youssef, and Philippe Fargues, *Chrétiens et Juifs dans l'Islam arabe et turc*, Fayard, 1992

Courbage, Youssef, and Emmanuel Todd, *Le rendez-vous des civilisations*, Editions du Seuil, 2007

Dalrymple, William, *From the Holy Mountain*, HarperCollins, 1997

De Botton, Alain, *The Consolations of Philosophy*, Hamish Hamilton, 2000

Debray, Régis, *Un Candide en Terre sainte*, Gallimard, 2008

Deltombe, Thomas, *L'islam imaginaire. La construction médiatique de l'islamophobie en France, 1975–2005*, La Découverte, 2005

Diamond, Jared, *Collapse: How Societies Choose to Fail or Survive*, Allen Lane, 2005

Enderlin, Charles, *Les années perdues: Intifada et guerres au Proche-Orient 2001–2006*, Fayard, 2006

Engelhard, Philippe, *L'homme mondial. Les sociétés humaines peuvent-elles survivre?*, Arléa, 1996

Fargues, Philippe, *Générations arabes. L'alchimie du nombre*, Fayard, 2001

Fernández-Armesto, Felipe, *Ideas That Changed the World*, Dorling Kindersley, 2003

Fisk, Robert, *The Great War for Civilisation: The Conquest of the Middle East*, Harper Perennial, 2006

Flannery, Tim, *The Weather Makers: The History and Future Impact of Climate Change*, Allen Lane, 2006

Friedman, Thomas, *The World Is Flat: A Brief History of the Globalized World in the Twenty-first Century*, Allen Lane, 2005

Fromkin, David, *A Peace to End All Peace: The Fall of the Ottoman Empire and the Creation of the Modern Middle East*, André Deutsch, 1989

Gifford, Rob, *China Road: A Journey into the Future of a Rising Power*, Bloomsbury, 2007

Girod, Michel, *Penser le racisme*, Calmann-Lévy, 2004

Gombrich, Ernst, *A Little History of the World*, Yale University Press, 2005

Grass, Günter, *Peeling the Onion*, Harvill Secker, 2007

Green, Dominic, *Three Empires on the Nile: The Victorian Jihad 1869–1899*, The Free Press, 2007

Greilsamer, Ilan, *La nouvelle histoire d'Israël*, Gallimard, 1998

Griffin, John Howard, *Black Like Me*, Collins, 1962

Haffner, Sebastian, *Defying Hitler: A Memoir*, Weidenfeld & Nicolson, 2002

Harford, Tim, *The Undercover Economist*, Little, Brown, 2006

Hawking, Stephen, *A Brief History of Time: From the Big Bang to Black Holes*, Bantam, 1988

Hersh, Seymour, *Chain of Command: The Road from 9/11 to Abu Ghraib*, HarperCollins, 2004

Hitti, Philip K., *History of the Arabs*, Macmillan, 1948

Horner, Christopher, *The Politically Incorrect Guide to Global Warming and Environmentalism*, Regnery (US), 2007

Hourani, Albert, *Histoire des peuples arabes*, Points Seuil, 1993

Huntington, Samuel, *The Clash of Civilizations and the Remaking of World Order*, Simon & Schuster (US), 1996

Hussein, Mahmoud, *Penser le Coran*, Grasset & Fasquelle, Paris, 2009

Johnson, Chalmers, *Blowback: The Costs and Consequences of American Empire*, Little, Brown, 2000

Johnson, Paul, *Modern Times: A History of the World from the 1920s to the 1990s*, Orion, 1992

Karnow, Stanley, *Vietnam: A History*, Century, 1983

Kepel, Gilles, *Terreur et martyre: Relever le défi de civilisation*, Flammarion, 2008

Kinzer, Stephen, *All the Shah's Men: An American Coup and the Roots of Middle East Terror*, Wiley, 2003

—, *Overthrow: America's Century of Regime Change from Hawaii to Iraq*, Times Books (US), 2006

Klein, Naomi, *The Shock Doctrine: The Rise of Disaster Capitalism*, Allen Lane, 2007

Kolbert, Elizabeth, *Field Notes from a Catastrophe: Man, Nature and Climate Change*, Bloomsbury, 2006

Kriegel, Blandine, *Etat de droit ou Empire?*, Bayard, 2002

Krugman, Paul, *The Conscience of a Liberal*, W.W. Norton & Co., 2007

Laroui, Fouad, *De l'islamisme: Une réfutation personnelle du totalitarisme religieux*, Robert Laffont, 2006

Laurens, Henry, *Orientales*, CNRS, 2004

Lehrer, Jonah, *Proust Was a Neuroscientist*, Houghton Mifflin (US), 2008

Levi, Primo, *A Tranquil Star: Unpublished Stories*, Penguin, 2007

Lewis, Anthony, *Freedom for the Thought That We Hate: A Biography of the First Amendment*, Perseus Running, 2007

Lewis, Bernard, *What Went Wrong? Western Impact and Middle Eastern Response*, Weidenfeld & Nicolson, 2002

Maalouf, Amin, *On Identity*, Harvill, 2000

—, *The Crusades Through Arab Eyes*, Saqi Essentials, 2006

MacMillan, Margaret, *Peacemakers: The Paris Conference of 1919 and Its Attempt to End War*, John Murray, 2001

Marcus, Amy Dockser, *Jerusalem 1913: The Origins of the Arab–Israeli Conflict*, Viking (US), 2007

Maugham, William Somerset, *The Summing Up*, Vintage Classics, 2010

McCoy, Alfred W., *A Question of Torture: CIA Interrogation, from the Cold War to the War on Terror*, Metropolitan Books (US), 2006

Méchoulan, Henry, *Etre juif à Amsterdam au temps de Spinoza*, Albin Michel, 1991

Mendell, David, *Obama: From Promise to Power*, HarperCollins (US), 2008

Meredith, Robyn, *The Elephant and the Dragon: The Rise of India and China and What It Means to All of Us*, W.W. Norton & Co., 2008

Miller, Judith, Stephen Engelberg and William Broad, *Germs: The Ultimate Weapon*, Simon & Schuster, 2001

Mitchell, B., and James L. Godfrey Garrett, *Europe since 1815*, Appleton-Century-Crofts (US), 1947

Moïsi, Dominique, and François Boisivon, *La géopolitique de l'émotion: Comment les cultures de peur, d'humiliation et d'espoir façonnent le monde*, Flammarion, 2008

Mortenson, Greg, and David Oliver Relin, *Three Cups of Tea: One Man's Extraordinary Journey to Promote Peace – One School at a Time*, Penguin, 2007

Nasr, Marlène, *Les Arabes et l'Islam vus par les manuels scolaires français*, Karthala, 2001

Navarro, Peter, *The Coming China Wars: Where They Will Be Fought and How They Will Be Won*, FT Press, 2007

Nye, Joseph, *Soft Power: The Means to Success in World Politics*, Public Affairs Books (US), 2004

O'Shea, Stephen, *Sea of Faith: Islam and Christianity in the Medieval Mediterranean World*, Profile Books, 2006

Obama, Barack H., *Dreams from my Father: A Story of Race and Inheritance*, Canongate, 2007

—, *Speech on Race: A More Perfect Union*, BN Publishing (US), 2008

—, *The Audacity of Hope: Thoughts on Reclaiming the American Dream*, Canongate, 2006

Oren, Michael B., *Power, Faith and Fantasy: America in the Middle East, 1776 to the Present*, W.W. Norton & Co., 2007

—, *Six Days of War: June 1967 and the Making of the Modern Middle East*, Oxford University Press, 2002

Packer, George, *The Assassins' Gate: America in Iraq*, Faber, 2006

Pan, Philip P., *Out of Mao's Shadow: The Struggle for the Soul of a New China*, Picador, 2008

Pollard, Justin, and Howard Reid, *The Rise and Fall of Alexandria: Birthplace of the Modern Mind*, Viking (US), 2007

Rand, Ayn, *Atlas Shrugged*, Signet Books, 1997

Randal, Jonathan, *Osama: The Making of a Terrorist*, Alfred A. Knopf (US), 2004

Ricks, Thomas E., *Fiasco: The American Military Adventure in Iraq*, Penguin Press, 2006

Roberts, J. M., *The Triumph of the West*, Phoenix, 2001

Roy, Olivier, *La Laïcité face à l'islam*, Stock, 2005

Russo, Gus, *Live by the Sword: The Secret War against Castro and the Death of JFK*, Bancroft Press (US), 1998

Salam, Nawaf, *La citoyenneté en pays d'Islam*, in *La condition libanaise*, Editions An-Nahar, 2001

Salamé, Ghassan, *Appels d'empire*, Fayard, 1996

—, *Quand l'Amérique refait le monde*, Fayard, 2005

Sebag-Montefiore, Simon, *Stalin: The Court of the Red Tsar*, Weidenfeld & Nicolson, 2003

Segev, Tom, *1967: Israel, the War and the Year that Transformed the Middle East*, Little, Brown, 2007

Shadid, Anthony, *Night Draws Near: Iraq's People in the Shadow of America's War*, Henry Holt & Co. (US), 2005

Suskind, Ron, *The One Percent Doctrine: Deep Inside America's Pursuit of Its Enemies Since 9/11*, Simon & Schuster, 2006

Taleb, Nassim Nicholas, *Le Cygne noir: La puissance de l'imprévisible*, Les Belles Lettres, 2008

Theroux, Paul, *Dark Star Safari: Overland from Cairo to Cape Town*, Hamish Hamilton, 2002

Todd, Emmanuel, *After the Empire: The Breakdown of the American Order*, Constable, 2004

Todorov, Tzvetan, *La littérature en peril*, Flammarion, 2006

—, *The Fear of Barbarians: Beyond the Clash of Civilizations*, University of Chicago Press, 2010

Toynbee, Arnold, *A Study of History*, Oxford University Press, 1987

—, *La grande aventure de l'humanité*, Payot, 1994.

Tuchman, Barbara W., *The Proud Tower: A Portrait of the World Before the War 1890–1914*, Hamish Hamilton, 1966

Védrine, Hubert, *Continuer l'Histoire*, Flammarion, 2008

Wade, Nicholas, *Before the Dawn: Recovering the Lost History of Our Ancestors*, Duckworth, 2007

Weiner, Tim, *Legacy of Ashes: The History of the CIA*, Allen Lane, 2007

Wikan, Unni, *Generous Betrayal: Politics of Culture in the New Europe*, University of Chicago Press, 2002

Williams, William Carlos, *The Collected Poems, Vols 1 & 2*, Penguin, 1976

Wood, Michael, *The Story of India*, BBC Books, 2007

Woodward, Bob, *Bush at War*, Simon & Schuster, 2002

Wright, Lawrence, *The Looming Tower: Al-Qaeda's Road to 9/11*, Allen Lane, 2006

Zakaria, Fareed, *The Future of Freedom: Illiberal Democracy at Home and Abroad*, W.W. Norton & Co., 2003

Zinn, Howard, *A People's History of the United States: 1492–Present*, Pearson/Longman, 2003

A NOTE ON THE AUTHOR

Amin Maalouf was born in Lebanon in 1949. A journalist
and director of the daily newspaper *An-Nahar*, he lived in
Beirut until the start of the civil war in 1975, when he left
for Paris with his family. His life straddles East and West
– he reads and writes in Arabic, but chooses to publish in
French. He refuses to be limited to one identity, either
Arab or French, but chooses to be both simultaneously.
A novelist, essayist and memoirist, he has won prestigious
prizes, including the 1993 Prix Goncourt and the 2010
Asturias Prize, and was nominated for the 2011
International Man Booker. His novels include *Leo Africanus*,
The Rock of Tanios, *Samarkand* and *Balthasar's Odyssey*,
which together with *The Crusades through Arab Eyes*, *On
Identity* and *Origins: A Memoir* have been translated into
more than forty languages. He lives in Paris.

A NOTE ON THE TRANSLATOR

George Miller is the translator of *No and Me* and
Underground Time by Delphine de Vigan. He is also
a regular translator for *Le Monde diplomatique*'s English-
language edition, and the translator of *Conversations with
My Gardener* by Henri Cueco and *Inside Al-Qaeda* by
Mohammed Sifaoui.

A NOTE ON THE TYPE

The text of this book is set in Bembo. This type was first used in 1495 by the Venetian printer Aldus Manutius for Cardinal Bembo's *De Aetna*, and was cut for Manutius by Francesco Griffo. It was one of the types used by Claude Garamond (1480–1561) as a model for his Romain de l'Université, and so it was the forerunner of what became standard European type for the following two centuries. Its modern form follows the original types and was designed for Monotype in 1929.